P9-DMR-804

Study Guide

Shannon M. Lynch

Western Illinois University

Abnormal Psychology

James Hansell

University of Michigan, Ann Arbor

Lisa Damour

John Carroll University

WILEY

JOHN WILEY & SONS, INC.

Cover Illustration: Carol C. Grobe

Copyright © 2005 John Wiley & Sons, Inc. All rights reserved.

No part of this publication may be reproduced, stored in a retrieval system or transmitted
in any form or by any means, electronic, mechanical, photocopying, recording, scanning
or otherwise, except as permitted under Sections 107 or 108 of the 1976 United States
Copyright Act, without either the prior written permission of the Publisher, or
authorization through payment of the appropriate per-copy fee to the Copyright
Clearance Center, Inc. 222 Rosewood Drive, Danvers, MA 01923, (978) 750-8400,
fax (978) 646-8600. Requests to the Publisher for permission should be addressed to the
Permissions Department, John Wiley & Sons, Inc., 111 River Street, Hoboken, NJ 07030,
(201) 748-6011, fax (201) 748-6008.

To order books or for customer service, please call 1-800-CALL-WILEY (225-5945).

ISBN 0-471-70774-0

Printed in the United States of America

10 9 8 7 6 5 4 3 2 1

Printed and bound by Malloy Lithographing, Inc.

Table of Contents

Chapter 1
Abnormal Psychology: The Core Concepts

Learning Objectives

- In determining whether a person's behavior is truly *abnormal*, it is important to consider the following core concepts: the context of the behavior, the continuum between normal and abnormal behavior, the role of cultural and historical relativism in defining abnormality, the advantages and disadvantages of assigning a diagnosis to the individual's behavior, the principle of multiple causality, and the connection between mind and body.

- *The importance of context in defining and understanding abnormality*
  - Examining the **context** or the environment and circumstances surrounding an individual at a given time helps us to *define* the extent to which the behavior seems abnormal. We expect a person who has been exposed to danger or who has lost a loved one to express more extreme emotions than someone who was startled by a loud noise or who had a minor disagreement with a significant other. When reactions seem extreme given the circumstances, we are more likely to label behavior abnormal.
  - We also consider an individual's **context** as a way to help us to *understand* or explain behavior. A person's recent experiences as well as demographic characteristics can help us to understand his or her behavior. Specific problems or abnormal behaviors are likely to be influenced by such characteristics as age, gender, ethnicity, and cultural affiliation.

- *The continuum between normal and abnormal behavior*
  - Most abnormal behaviors are exaggerated or more extreme expressions of normal behaviors. In other words, behavior exists on a **continuum from normal to abnormal**. Because most people have experienced mild depression or anxiety, deciding when a behavior is actually abnormal can be challenging and the dividing line between normality and abnormality is not always clear.

- *Cultural and historical relativism in defining and classifying abnormality*
  - Definitions and classifications of abnormal behavior vary considerably across different cultures and across different historical periods. As a result, we cannot make absolute, universal statements about what constitutes abnormal behavior; we must consider the cultural and historical lens through which we view human behavior.

- *The advantages and limitations of diagnosis*
  - Psychologists use diagnostic categories with specific descriptive criteria to arrive at a diagnosis. Our goal as scientists is to create reliable or consistent and valid or accurate descriptions such that the same individual would receive the same diagnosis from different evaluators. Reliable and valid of diagnoses guide research and

improve our understanding of and ability to treat specific disorders. However, diagnostic labels can also be stigmatizing and lead to mistreatment by others.

- *The principle of multiple causality*
  - o Usually there are multiple causes for behavior, such as a combination of current circumstances (precipitating causes) and past experiences (predisposing causes). We also take into account biological (e.g., genetic predisposition) and psychological factors (traumatic event) in trying to explain abnormal behavior. Furthermore, we may find a combination of various theoretical explanations helpful in our efforts to determine why abnormal behavior occurs. In this way, we avoid reductionism or the oversimplification of people's experiences by relying on only one way to understand a problem.

- *The connection between mind and body*
  - o Emotional experiences influence our biological functioning (neurotransmitters, hormone levels, etc.) and vice versa. The mind and body are interacting, not separate and distinct entities.

Key Terms

- Reliability p. 6
- Validity p. 6
- Precipitating causes p. 6
- Predisposing causes p. 6
- Reductionism p. 7

Concept Questions

- How does context help us to define whether behavior is abnormal?
- Why do we take demographic variables such as age, gender, ethnicity, and cultural beliefs into account in trying to explain abnormal behavior?
- Have you ever been a little depressed or anxious? How do we decide when such feelings are "abnormal?"
- What are some advantages of using diagnostic labels? Limitations?
- Why must we strive to develop valid and reliable diagnostic categories? What would happen if our diagnostic system was invalid and unreliable?
- What is the difference between a precipitating cause and a predisposing cause?
- What is reductionism and why is it problematic?

Multiple-Choice Questions

1. To define and understand abnormal behavior, it is critical to consider all of the following except
    A. life circumstances
    B. demographic characteristics
    C. only one perspective or theory
    D. the continuum between normal and abnormal behavior
    Ans. C

2. Valid diagnostic criteria are
    A. accurate
    B. reliable
    C. specific
    D. accountable
    Ans. A

3. Recently Jen was in an automobile accident and now she has panic attacks whenever she has to drive. The auto accident is an example of a
    A. predisposing cause of the panic attacks
    B. precipitating cause of the panic attacks
    C. preexisting cause of the panic attacks
    D. reductionism
    Ans. B

Short-Answer Essay Questions

1. How do we decide whether someone's behavior is abnormal? What factors would you want to take into consideration?

2. Tim is 8 years old and has gotten in trouble all year for talking in class, not doing his work, and getting out of his seat. A brief interview with Tim and his mother reveals that Tim's father left for Iraq just before school started and the family is having financial difficulties; Tim's older brother has been diagnosed with attention deficit hyperactivity disorder, and Tim has a history of some acting out in the classroom, (but this recent behavior is the worst behavior he has ever exhibited). Discuss how each of the core concepts might help you to define and explain Tim's behavior.

Chapter 2
Defining Abnormality: What is Psychopathology?

Learning Objectives

Commonly used criteria for defining abnormality
- Several different criteria have been proposed for use in defining abnormality, but there is no absolute or exact definition of psychopathology.
- One possibility is to define abnormality based on whether individuals seek help for their problems. Although help–seeking does suggest an individual is suffering in some way, a problem with using this as a criterion is that not all individuals with abnormal behavior seek treatment or assistance, and many people seek help for "normal" stressors rather than for behavior we would categorize as abnormal.
- A second criterion used to evaluate whether behavior is abnormal is the degree to which a person appears out-of-control, irrational, or dangerous. However, the majority of individuals with mental illness are not violent, or out of control.
- Deviance or extremely usual behavior is a third criterion that can be used to determine abnormality. However, some deviant behavior is unusual in that it is extremely advantageous and occurs in emotionally stable people, such as some talented athletes or musicians. In addition, many people who suffer from milder disorders may not appear to be deviant and thus would not receive treatment if we relied on this definition alone.
- Emotional distress—suffering—is one way we often define abnormality and is generally considered more useful than help–seeking, irrational/out-of-control behavior, or deviance. However, not everyone who is mentally ill feels distress and many people who feel distress are not exhibiting abnormal behavior.
- The final criterion is significant impairment of functioning. Often, this is considered the best indicator of abnormality but it is important to note that: physical problems can also cause impaired psychological functioning; not everyone who meets criteria for abnormal behavior is substantially impaired in their ability to function; and finally, people have different ideas about what it means to have impaired functioning.
- Using the five criteria together (HIDES) is generally considered the most effective means of defining behavior as abnormal.

Core concepts in defining abnormality
- The type of behavior we consider to be normal or abnormal varies widely across different cultures and in different periods of history. The concepts of *cultural and historical relativism* are critical in defining abnormality given that behavior may be considered abnormal *relative* to the beliefs and customs of a particular culture and in a given era or historical period.
- The *continuum between normal and abnormal behavior* makes it very challenging to pinpoint an exact definition of abnormality. Most of us experience some form of at least some of the symptoms or problems described in the *DSM-IV-TR*. In fact, it is common for students in abnormal psychology to recognize behaviors or feelings listed in the diagnostic criteria as ones that are familiar in their own lives. It is only when one meets the specified

number of criteria, is in distress, and/or has impaired functioning that we consider the behavior or experience to be abnormal.

Defining abnormality: practical solutions
- Behavior is typically labeled using *working definitions* such as from the *DSM* rather than each individual clinician struggling to evaluate a person on the basis of the five criteria discussed above. Although working definitions are not perfect, they work well enough in everyday use that we can generally identify when behavior is abnormal.
- Currently, definitions for different diagnosis are based on descriptive criteria listed in the *Diagnostic and Statistical Manual of Mental Disorders* (*DSM*). Each new edition of the *DSM* describes the currently accepted criteria or standards for diagnosing hundreds of disorders. It is important to note that the authors of the *DSM* specifically state that the categories remain imprecise or *fuzzy*, and that the criteria of distress and impairment are critical considerations in the diagnostic process.

Key Terms

- Abnormal psychology p. 11
- Psychopathology p. 11
- Natural categories p. 23

Concept Questions

- Why do many people believe help–seeking should be considered a criterion for abnormality? What is a disadvantage of using the presence or absence of help–seeking to define abnormality?
- What happened when Rosenhan and his colleagues began acting "normally" in the hospital? Why is the outcome of Rosenhan's study important?
- Why should we consider **context** when evaluating dangerousness or "out of control behavior"?
- How do we categorize someone who expresses an opinion that differs from the majority opinion? When is a different or unusual worldview an example of abnormality and when is it not?
- What is an advantage of using the emotional distress criterion? A limitation?
- What is significant impairment? How precisely can we define this term?
- What are the five criteria for defining abnormality which are include in the acronym HIDES?
- What is medical student's syndrome? How does this concept apply to students taking abnormal psychology?
- What are natural categories and how do we use them to determine whether behavior is abnormal?
- What are the main points emphasized by the authors of the *DSM* in their discussion of working definitions of mental disorders?

Multiple-Choice Questions

1. Rosenhan and his colleagues conducted a famous study in which they presented themselves to a psychiatric hospital, saying they heard voices, but began acting normally as soon as they were admitted to the hospital. The findings from this study illustrate some of the problems regarding
    A. including distress in the definition of abnormality
    B. including impaired functioning in the definition of abnormality
    C. relying on help-seeking behavior as a primary indicator of mental illness
    D. psychologists who use deception in their studies
    Ans. C

2. In Latin culture, falling in love has been equated with being in an irrational, out-of-control state. This suggests the importance of considering _____ when developing criteria to define abnormal behavior.
    A. context
    B. distress
    C. impairment
    D. help seeking
    Ans. A

3. Ace is a strange person. He refuses to talk, he walks for several hours each day, and he eats only macaroni and cheese. No one knows what is wrong with him, but he appears abnormal. What criterion are people in his community *most* likely to use to define his behavior as abnormal?
    A. help seeking
    B. irrationality/dangerousness
    C. deviance
    D. emotional distress
    Ans. C

4. Homosexuality was considered abnormal behavior and was, at one time, classified in the *DSM*. Later, it was removed from the *DSM* owing to a combination of scientific findings and political and social changes. This shift in defining a gay or lesbian sexual orientation as normal demonstrates
    A. cultural relativism
    B. historical relativism
    C. the advantages and disadvantages of diagnoses
    D. the mind body connection
    Ans. B

5. Working definitions of abnormality are
    A. precise lists of criteria based on proven facts
    B. best represented by help seeking, irrationality, and deviance
    C. loose descriptions of how people's functioning can be impaired in love and at work
    D. based on natural categories and generally effective in identifying abnormal behavior
    Ans. D

Short-Answer Essay Questions

1. Describe each of the five criteria offered as tools for defining abnormal behavior and note a strength and a weakness of each criterion.

2. According to Rosenhan and Szasz, what is the role of social context in creating and maintaining abnormal behavior?

3. What is cultural relativism and how is it relevant to diagnosis?

4. What prevents us from having a universal definition of abnormality?

5. How precise are our working definitions for abnormality? What rationales do experts use for accepting imprecise definitions of abnormality?

Chapter 3
Explaining Abnormality: What Causes Psychopathology?

Learning Objectives

Explaining abnormality: The core concepts

Cultural and historical relativism

- Throughout recorded history, people have attempted to understand or explain abnormal behavior. Very early explanations of abnormality relied on the concept of animism or the idea that abnormal behavior was caused by possession by an evil spirit. Although this explanation may seem bizarre, at the time it was culturally relevant because beliefs in spirits were commonly used to explain many events and experiences. In Greek and Roman times, physicians and philosophers argued that psychopathology was caused by biological problems such as an imbalance among four essential fluids (black bile, yellow bile, blood, and phlegm) or a wandering uterus.

- Attempts to explain abnormality have shifted among several different paradigms over the centuries: spiritual, biological, and psychological. Although various explanations have been made over the years, the tendency has been to rely on only one theory to explain abnormal behavior (reductionism) in a given time period. This tendency can result in oversimplified explanations and prevent us from recognizing the complexity of an individual's experience. This is why abnormal behavior is generally best explained by combining multiple theories.

The connection between mind and body

- Current psychological explanations of abnormal behavior focus on including both mind and body. Although these explanations emphasize that some disorders are more likely to be caused by psychological factors, while others are influenced by biological factors, most disorders are influenced by both mind and body.

The theoretical perspectives

- The psychodynamic perspective emphasizes unconscious processes, emotional conflict, and early childhood experiences. Sigmund Freud was an early theorist and psychoanalyst who is considered one of the major contributors to this theoretical perspective. For example, he developed a theory of the psyche as divided into the id, ego, and superego and described how people avoided unacceptable thoughts and feelings through the use of repression. Freud and his followers used his theories to describe many types of defense mechanisms or unconscious processes that we use to lessen the anxiety provoked by emotional conflict. Several of Freud's followers subsequently expanded or developed new theories based on his work. These include the Kleinian school of thought, object-relations theory, and self-psychology. In general, psychodynamic treatment is aimed at helping clients achieve insight into their conflicts and work through them in order to change maladaptive behavioral patterns.

- Similar to some psychodynamic theorists, humanistic theories also focus on important relationships, but place a greater emphasis on current interpersonal connections as well as the freedom to make choices that help an individual reach his or her greatest potential.

Theorists in this perspective argue that psychopathology occurs when individuals are prevented from reaching their full potential, which is most likely to occur if they have to meet certain conditions in order to receive the love and support of others. Therapists in this tradition use empathy and active listening to help their clients regain or develop greater self-regard.

- Existential theorists emphasize the critical significance of accepting responsibility for personal choices. In particular, these theorists note the importance of confronting dilemmas and striving to be realistic in order to be emotionally healthy.
- Behaviorism stresses learning—both voluntary and involuntary—and argues that abnormal behavior can be explained by observable, testable procedures rather than hypothesizing about the existence of internal or unconscious processes. Classical conditioning is learning that takes place when a neutral stimulus is paired with an unconditioned stimulus that elicits a particular response. Operant conditioning posits that behaviors that are rewarded increase and behaviors that are punished decrease. Behaviorists also note that learning can take place by observing others such as through modeling or social learning. Some examples of behavioral treatment principles include counterconditioning, systematic desensitization, aversion therapy, contingency management, token economies, and social skills training.
- An individual's thoughts and beliefs are central to the cognitive perspective. Cognitive theorists highlight ways in which individuals distort or misinterpret their experiences. Identifying and discussing a client's attributions or beliefs about the causes of events and then helping him/her to develop more realistic schemas are the main goals of cognitive treatment.
- Sociocultural theorists propose that abnormal behavior occurs in response to social pressures, such as the pressure for people to be thin, and cultural forces, such as a lack of financial resources. Thus, to prevent abnormal behavior, proponents of this perspective argue for changes within the larger community or culture.
- Family systems theorists view abnormal behavior within the *context* of the family. They view extreme in closeness or distance among family members as well as the need to maintain the current state of the family as causes for individual difficulties. They argue that family members have expectations of the roles each person will fill and at times, these expectations place undue stress or pressure on individuals within the family. Family therapists work with the entire family in order to change the ways the family members interact with one another.
- The biological perspective focuses on structural abnormalities or chemical imbalances (particularly in the brain) as causes of abnormal behavior. Influences that lead to these abnormalities may be biological (particular combination of genes) and/or environmental (lead poisoning). Biological treatments are aimed at the body and most often involve medications that change the balance of various neurotransmitters in the brain.

Key Terms

- Animism p. 30
- Deinstitutionalization p. 32
- Humours p. 33
- Hysteria p. 33
- Suggestion p. 34

- Lobotomy p. 69
- Insulin coma p. 69
- Electroshock therapy p. 69
- Psychotropic p. 69
- Agonists p. 69
- Antagonists p. 69
- Psychotic p. 70
- Delusions p. 70
- Hallucinations p. 70

Concept Questions

- What is trephination? How is this an example of animism?
- What biological theories did early Greeks and Romans rely on to explain abnormal behavior?
- Describe moral treatment and indicate how this form of treatment differed from earlier care for the mentally ill.
- What is the diathesis–stress model? How does it combine psychological and biological perspectives?
- Discuss the three main principles that argue for the importance of including the *mind–body connection* in our explanation of abnormal behavior.
- What is psychodynamic theory? How does it differ from psychoanalytic theory?
- Why did Freud and his colleagues find hypnosis such a useful tool? How was hypnosis used therapeutically?
- What was Freud's structural theory of the mind?
- What is projection? How does projection differ from reaction formation?
- What is the main focus in the Kleinian school of thought?
- What is the importance of the relationship with early caregivers in object-relational theory? Discuss how this theory draws connections between early relationships and later behavior.
- What is the role of parenting in Kohut's theory of self-psychology?
- Describe transference and countertransference. How might these processes influence treatment from a psychodynamic perspective?
- What is unconditional positive regard? How do "conditions of worth" interfere with self-actualization?
- What does it mean to be inauthentic from the existentialist perspective? How does this relate to pathology?
- When is the best time to introduce the conditioned stimulus—before or after the unconditioned stimulus?
- What is the difference between positive and negative reinforcement? How does negative reinforcement differ from punishment?
- Give an example of social or observational learning. How does this concept differ from operant conditioning?
- What is counterconditioning?
- When might a therapist employ exposure as a treatment strategy?
- What are some common cognitive distortions?

- What is an empirically supported treatment? What is an advantage of this form of treatment? A disadvantage?
- How does the sociocultural perspective explain the presence of abnormal behaviors? What do sociocultural theorists believe leads to abnormal behaviors?
- What is the difference between an enmeshed family and a disengaged one?
- What is a double-bind message? How would double-bind messages influence the way a child learns to relate to others?
- Describe the components of the autonomic nervous system. How do these two systems work in conjunction with one another?
- Why do we study twins and adopted children to learn about abnormal behavior from the biological perspective?

Multiple-Choice Questions

1. Experiencing temporary symptoms in various areas of the body, such as loss of feeling in an arm followed by leg pains was labeled as _____ by early Greek physicians.
   A. hysteria
   B. paradigms
   C. animism
   D. trephination
   Ans. A

2. Jane has been feeling very anxious ever since a tornado damaged several houses on her street a few weeks ago. She has been worried about leaving her house and has trouble sleeping. She knows that several of her relatives have had anxiety disorders but she never felt that she might have one until recently. Jane's experience is best explained by
   A. psychodynamic theory
   B. the diathesis-stress model
   C. general paresis
   D. cognitive theory
   Ans. B

3. According to Freud, children are most likely to be struggling with issues of control and autonomy during the _____ phase.
   A. oral
   B. anal
   C. phallic
   D. latency
   Ans. B

4. Eric is very angry with his little brother who took his favorite G.I. Joe toy and then lost it. Eric knows he will get in trouble if he yells at his brother so he yelled at his puppy even though it didn't do anything wrong. This is an example of
   A. reaction formation
   B. projection
   C. rationalization
   D. displacement
   Ans. D

5. Stacy is very excited because she has been accepted to the college of her choice. She wants to tell her parents but is afraid they will say that if she goes to school in a far away state, she will disappoint certain family members so much that they won't attend her high school graduation. In this example, Stacy seems to be experiencing which of the following?
   A. conditions of worth
   B. empathy
   C. projection
   D. instrumental conditioning
   Ans. A

6. Tim always hits the snooze button when his alarm goes off. The relief Tim feels when he hits the snooze button is an example of
   A. a conditioned stimulus
   B. an unconditioned response
   C. positive reinforcement
   D. negative reinforcement
   Ans. D

7. The weakening of a connection between a conditioned stimulus and a conditioned response is called _____.
   A. contingency management
   B. shaping
   C. extinction
   D. punishment
   Ans. C

8. Sandy always focuses on what goes wrong. She threw a party for a friend last week—the food was good, lots of people came, and everyone seemed to have fun. But Sandy thought it was a disaster because it rained and they couldn't celebrate outside as she had planned. Sandy is demonstrating which of the following?
   A. countertransference
   B. conditions of worth
   C. overgeneralization
   D. selective abstraction
   Ans. D

9. Which of the following is the best predictor of therapeutic outcome?
   A. therapeutic alliance
   B. socioeconomic status
   C. empirically supported treatment
   D. level of client engagement
   Ans. A

10. Family systems theorists argue that family members are often motivated to maintain
_____ even if it causes problems for certain family members.
A. cognitive triad
B. imbalance
C. homoeostasis
D. overgeneralization
Ans. C

11. Neurotransmitters are released into the _____ after an impulse travels down the axon
and reaches the axon terminals.
A. cell body
B. synaptic cleft
C. dendrites
D. basal ganglia
Ans. B

12. The _____ helps to regulate the endocrine system.
A. hypothalamus
B. thalamus
C. peripheral nervous system
D. frontal lobe
Ans. A

Short-Answer Essay Questions

1. Describe a spiritual, a psychological, and a biological explanation of abnormality from earlier historical times. Why do you think these explanations were accepted at those times?

2. What is a paradigm? Why do paradigms change?

3. How does the principle of *multiple causality* help us to understand conditions such as general paresis or psychosocial dwarfism?

4. What is the purpose of a defense mechanism? Identify and describe three defense mechanisms. Give an example of each.

5. Compare and contrast three contemporary perspectives within psychodynamic theory. Can you think of an example of how it might be helpful to use these different perspectives together, as is suggested by the principle of *multiple causality*?

6. How are the actions of others important in the process of self-actualization?

7. Compare and contrast the importance of relationships from a behavioral perspective (such as through modeling) versus a humanist perspective.

8. Discuss the concept of explanatory styles and give an example of how one's explanatory style might influence one's thoughts about the break up of an important relationship.

9. How are family systems theorists and sociocultural theorists alike? How do they differ, particularly in terms of their treatment approaches?

10. Draw and label a neuron and describe the process by which it fires.

11. Discuss different types of evidence for genetic contributions to some disorders.

Chapter 4
Classifying Abnormality: Diagnosis and Assessment

Learning Objectives

Diagnosis
- Psychologists and other mental health professionals classify abnormal behavior into diagnostic categories or diagnoses. Clear communications about abnormal behavior is essential so that we can better determine the causes of different disorders and develop effective treatments through research and practice.
- In general, scientists determine the effectiveness of their classification systems by examining the reliability and validity of the categories. As we discussed previously, a concept or test is reliable if it is consistent, and it is valid if it is accurate.
- In the mental health field, professionals need to be able to reliably apply diagnostic criteria such that different treaters give an individual who presents certain symptoms the same diagnosis. Similarly, questionnaires designed to aid diagnosis should provide reliable or consistent results.
- Clinical interviews or questionnaires need to produce results that are valid or accurate. To increase validity, the criteria for many of the diagnosis are very specific. For example, many diagnoses require that an individual display at least a certain number of symptoms and that they report experiencing these problems for specified periods of time. However, many people who seek treatment report symptoms that seem to fit into general diagnostic categories but fail to meet all of the specified requirements. Thus a current controversy in the field centers around whether we should rely on a categorical diagnostic system (like the *DSM*) or a dimensional system that assesses the degree to which individuals experience particular symptoms.
- The *DSM* has changed dramatically over time. The first *Diagnostic and Statistical Manual of Mental Disorders* was published in 1952 and listed 108 diagnoses. Currently, there are more than 300 diagnoses with specific criteria or guidelines listed in the *Diagnostic and Statistical Manual of Mental Disorders- IV-TR (DSM)*.
- In addition, substantial changes in the third edition of the *DSM* led to a greater emphasis on specific descriptive criteria that are atheoretical in nature. These changes were made to increase validity and reliability of the diagnoses, but critics suggest that there are still many problems regarding reliability and validity as well as theoretical and cultural biases. Although controversy about the *DSM* system continues, it is widely used by clinicians and researchers.
- The *DSM* outlines a multiaxial system for making a diagnosis. Axis I is where the most common disorders, symptom-based disorders, are listed. Axis II is the location designated for long-term, pervasive disorders such as personality disorders. Medical conditions that may relate to abnormal behavior (such as a head injury if a person is exhibiting changes in personality) are listed on Axis III. Axis IV is used to indicate whether the person has experienced recent stressors (such as a job loss). Finally, Axis V is used to convey the severity of the person's impairment in functioning. Mental health professionals record a

number based on the Global Assessment of Functioning scale (GAF) which indicates how the individual is functioning and can be used to assess progress over time.

Assessment

- To gather information relevant to making a diagnosis, clinicians and researchers use three primary tools: interviews, tests, and observations.
- Interviews are either standardized ones in which the clinician follows a specific series of questions or instructions (structured) or more exploratory, allowing flexibility in determining which questions would be most useful in a given situation (unstructured). Structured interviews generally are reliable when used by trained clinicians and typically are used to determine if a person meets specific criteria for a disorder. Unstructured interviews allow the interviewer to not only gather information but also to learn more about the person's experiences–how and why the person might feel as he or she does. This flexibility may compromise reliability. Many clinicians and researchers use a semi-structured interview, combining elements of each style, to increase both reliability and validity.
- Many assessment tools exist. Some are specifically designed to assess for the presence and severity of symptoms for specific diagnoses such as the Beck Depression Inventory, whereas others are more general personality tests such as the Minnesota Multiphasic Personality Inventory. Measures such as these typically provide good reliability and moderate validity.
- Projective tests such as the Rorschach Inkblot test are typically considered less reliable and valid; however, they are more descriptive of the individual client in that they assess deeper, less obvious emotional processes.
- Other assessment tools include achievements tests, neuropsychological tests, biological tests, and behavioral observations.
- A good assessment leads not only to a clear diagnosis but also provides the clinician with a greater overall understanding of the individual. A diagnosis alone is often insufficient to determine the origin of a person's problem and the most effective means of treating the problems.

Key Terms

Concept Questions

- How can we determine if a diagnostic interview or questionnaire is reliable?
- When is a diagnosis valid?
- How did the *DSM* develop?
- What are some criticisms of the recent editions of the *DSM*?
- What is the difference between Axis I and II?
- On which Axis would a psychologist note that a person recently lost a parent or a partner?
- What is the purpose of the GAF? How can this number be used to measure change over time?
- What is the difference between a structured and an unstructured interview? What are the goals of each type of interview?
- What are the advantages and disadvantages of using symptom-based measures such as the BDI or personality inventories such as the MMPI?
- How do projective tests differ from tests such as the MMPI? What is a strength of projective tests? A limitation?
- For what purpose might a clinician use a Draw-A-Person test?
- What was the purpose of the Stanford-Binet when it was first developed?
- What does an intelligence test consist of and what is it typically used for?
- How do we use tests to assess if someone has a learning disability?
- What can neuropsychological tests tell us about abnormal behavior?
- What are biological tests used for? Why might we expect use of these tests to increase?
- When might it be useful to include a behavioral observation in an assessment?
- What are the ultimate goals of the assessment process?

Multiple-Choice Questions

1. Diagnosis is to _____ as assessment is to _____.
   A. classification; gathering information
   B. gathering information; classification
   C. testing; interviewing
   D. interviewing; testing
   Ans. A

2. Questionnaires that reliably diagnose depression
   A. are accurate
   B. are proven to be true
   C. consistently rate the same individuals as depressed
   D. are never as accurate as being interviewed by a trained professional
   Ans. C

3. The *DSM-III* differed from previous editions in that the authors
   A. created complex flow charts so that every individual could be diagnosed based on the severity of his or her symptoms
   B. emphasized theoretical explanations of the cause of each disorder
   C. used simplified criteria that was primarily descriptive and atheoretical
   D. decided to use a psychodynamic orientation to explain each disorder in terms of unconscious motivations and emotional conflicts
   Ans. C

4. Will has been in and out of treatment for many years. He has been told he has long-standing problems in his interactions with others but he doesn't agree—he believes he has had a lot of impatient and uncaring employers, friends, and relatives. Based on this description, on what axis is his therapist most likely to list a diagnosis?
   A. Axis I
   B. Axis II
   C. Axis III
   D. Axis IV
   Ans. B

5. The Global Assessment of Functioning (GAF) scale is
   A. a measure of how many different diagnoses an individual has
   B. a measure of Axis I versus Axis II symptoms
   C. a measure of associated physical problems
   D. a measure of the severity of impairment
   Ans. D

6. Dr. Paul is interested in assessing the severity of various specific problems associated with depression that a new client is experiencing. Thus, he decides to administer a _____ to his new client.
   A. symptom inventory
   B. personality inventory
   C. projective test
   D. unstructured interview
   Ans. A.

7. Intelligence tests are typically used for all of the following reasons except
   A. to diagnose learning problems when used in conjunction with others tests
   B. to assess general intellectual ability and functioning
   C. to determine the presence or absence of a personality disorder
   D. to ascertain whether an individual meets the criteria for mental retardation
   Ans. C

8. Mark's parents and teachers have agreed to note each time he complies with a direct instruction and each time he does not. The therapist working with them has asked them to also note what happened just after he complied or did not comply with a direct request. The therapist is using _____ in his assessment of Mark.
   A. classical conditioning
   B. behavioral observations
   C. negative reinforcement
   D. neuropsychological tests
   Ans. B

9. Biological tests are currently _____ form of assessment in the field of abnormal psychology.
   A. an infrequent
   B. the most frequent
   C. the preferred
   D. an obsolete
   Ans. A

Short-Answer Essay Questions

1. Why do we emphasize developing and using valid diagnoses? What are the disadvantages of improving the accuracy of our diagnostic categories by making them highly specific?

2. What are Dr. McHugh's criticisms of modern psychiatry? Do you agree or disagree with his perspective regarding the increased reliance on medications to treat psychological disorders?

3. What are some advantages and disadvantages of the current *DSM* approach?

4. Describe the five axes of the multiaxial system and note what content goes on each axis.

5. Describe at least three steps a psychologist might take to assess a teenager whose parents report the following concerns: problems in schools, frequent disagreements with family members, increased isolation from friends in the past year, and a recent increase in his expression of anger. Why might they use each assessment tool or technique?

6. What steps or tools might a psychologist include in an assessment process to not only reach a diagnosis, but to better understand a client?

Chapter 5
Anxiety and the Anxiety Disorders

Learning Objectives

Defining anxiety and the anxiety disorders
- Anxiety, an unpleasant sensation in response to a perceived threat, is a normal part of life.
- Fear differs from anxiety in that it is a response to a specific danger.
- Your body has a normal physiological response to perceived threats that includes increased heart rate, pupil dilation, perspiration, and dry mouth.
- In general, anxiety can consist of emotional, cognitive, physical, and behavioral responses.
- Anxiety can occur on a continuum from mild to intense and is defined as abnormal when it is extreme or irrational given its specific *context* and so intense that it causes substantial distress and/or impairs an individual's functioning.
- A person who has trait anxiety tends to respond to many different situations with anxiety. In contrast, state anxiety takes place in response to a specific situation or threat.
- Too little anxiety can also place a person at risk for engaging in abnormal behavior. Individuals who experience low levels of arousal in normal contexts may seek out risky situations to reach an optimal level of arousal.
- In general, a moderate level of anxiety helps an individual maintain concentration but does not impair his/her competence.

Classifying anxiety and the anxiety disorders
- Anxiety disorders are those in which the predominant or main symptom a person experiences is intense anxiety.
- There are six anxiety disorders: generalized anxiety disorder, panic disorder, phobias, obsessive-compulsive disorder, posttraumatic stress disorder, and acute stress disorder.
- Generalized anxiety disorder consists of a chronic anxiety (tension or worry) that is experienced in most or all *contexts* for at least six months.
- Panic disorder occurs when an individual experiences a panic attack—a period of intense symptoms such as rapid heart rate, sweating, shaking or shortness of breath—and then changes his/her behavior because of a fear of having additional attacks.
- A specific (or simple) phobia is an irrational fear of an object or situation that influences one's behavior and/or evokes intense anxiety when the individual confronts the feared stimulus.
- Social phobia occurs when the feared stimulus is a social situation or activity where one anticipates being judged by others.
- Agoraphobia is the fear of having a panic attack in a public place where one may have difficulty escaping or getting help.
- Specific phobias are most likely to be fears of animals, aspects of the environment (e.g., height), blood or injury, or certain situations (e.g., flying, or confined space).
- Obsessive-compulsive disorder consists of frequent, unwanted thoughts and ritualized behaviors that decrease anxiety brought on by intrusive thoughts.

- An obsession is a recurrent thought or image that is inappropriate and/or unwanted, which causes anxiety.
- A compulsion is a behavior a person feels compelled to perform to reduce or alleviate anxiety.
- Posttraumatic stress disorder is only diagnosed when an individual experiences or witnesses a life-threatening event and then experiences intrusive symptoms (e.g., nightmares or flashbacks), numbing symptoms such as feeling of detachment, and increased arousal for more than a month after the event.
- Acute stress disorder is diagnosed when a person experiences posttraumatic symptoms within a month of a life-threatening event.

Classification in demographic context
- Symptoms of anxiety differ depending on a person's age.
- Females report symptoms of anxiety disorders two to three times more often then men. This gender difference has been explained in terms of sociocultural, hormonal, and genetic factors.
- Individuals in lower income groups are at greater risk for developing anxiety disorders.
- Cultural context is an important consideration when applying the *DSM-IV-TR* diagnostic categories; individuals from different cultures report differing experiences of anxiety.

Explaining and treating the anxiety disorders
- Behavioral theories based on classical conditioning, operant conditioning, and modeling offer insight into how anxiety disorders, particularly phobias, develop.
- One explanation for some common phobias is that humans are evolutionarily prepared to fear stimuli such as specific animals or situations that once posed serious threats to our survival.
- Exposure therapies are common and effective interventions used to treat anxiety disorders. Exposure can be to actual (in vivo) or imagined (covert) stimuli and direct or via the therapist (modeling). The most extreme form of exposure is flooding.
- Cognitive theorists propose that anxiety arises when the individual is preoccupied with the potential threat and underestimates his/her ability to cope with the threat. This results in cognitive distortions such as catastrophizing, dichotomous reasoning, personalization, and labeling.
- Cognitive interventions are designed to help clients identify distortions in their schemas and then to join the therapist in a collaborative effort to evaluate and challenge maladaptive assumptions and beliefs.
- In general, theorists from the biological perspective focus on how anxiety disorders are associated with the functioning of the autonomic system, the limbic system, and neurotransmitters such as norepinephrine, serotonin, and GABA. They also note that substantial genetic evidence suggests that individuals are at greater risk of developing an anxiety disorder if they have first-degree relatives with an anxiety disorder.
- The sympathetic nervous system activates the body in response to threats, while the parasympathetic nervous system returns the body to a calm, relaxed state.
- Biological treatments for panic attacks consist of antidepressants such as SSRIs or tricyclics which work by inhibiting reuptake of certain neurotransmitters. SSRIs are also used to treat OCD and PTSD. Benzodiazepines, beta-blockers, and azaspirones are used to treat some

anxiety disorders as well, although it is important to note the addictive properties of some benzodiazapenes limit use of these medications to short periods of time.

- Psychodynamic theorists propose that anxiety disorders occur when an individual cannot tolerate an internal conflict and subsequently uses defense mechanisms, such as projection, to reduce or manage anxiety. Some psychodynamic theorists emphasize the role of disrupted or problematic early parent-child relationships in the development of an anxiety disorder. Psychodynamic interventions are aimed at identifying and addressing the under-lying causing conflict.
- In most cases, two or more types of interventions are combined to treat anxiety disorders most effectively.

Key Terms

- Anxiety p. 111
- Trait anxiety p. 113
- State anxiety p. 113
- Generalized anxiety disorder p. 115
- Panic disorder p. 116
- Phobia p. 117
- Social phobia p. 118
- Agoraphobia p. 118
- Specific phobia p. 119
- Obsessive-compulsive disorder p. 119
- Obsession p. 119
- Compulsion p. 119
- Trauma p. 122
- Acute stress disorder p. 122
- Posttraumatic stress disorder p. 122
- Flashback p. 124
- Comorbidity p. 125
- Nervios p. 128
- Ataque de Nervios p. 129
- Shenjing Shuairuo p. 129
- Taijin Kyofusho p. 129
- Classical conditioning p. 131
- Operant conditioning p. 131
- Modeling p. 131
- Temporal contiguity p. 132
- Negative reinforcement p. 132
- Extinction p. 132
- Vicarious conditioning p. 132
- Prepared conditioning p. 132
- Systematic desensitization p. 133
- Relaxation training p. 133
- Fear herarchy p. 133
- In vivo desensitization p. 133

Concept Questions

- What is a normal physiological response to fear?
- Why is the *context* important in determining whether anxiety is normal or abnormal? Give an example in which anxiety would be an abnormal response.
- Describe the difference between state and trait anxiety.
- Can a person experience too little anxiety? What are the possible repercussions of feeling too little anxiety?

- What is the ideal level of anxiety? Why is this level predictive of successful outcomes?
- Why might some people be drawn to activities such as sky diving, rock climbing, mountain biking, or cliff diving?
- What is the difference between someone who worries a lot and someone with generalized anxiety disorder?
- Why do many people mistakenly believe they are having a heart attack when they experience their first panic attack?
- What are the differences among specific phobia, social phobia, and agoraphobia? How are these disorders similar?
- Why do individuals with obsessive-compulsive disorder (OCD) engage in compulsive behaviors? How are compulsions related to obsessions?
- Give an example of an intrusive symptom as opposed to a numbing symptom of posttraumatic stress disorder (PTSD).
- How does social support influence the development of a disorder such as PTSD or acute stress disorder?
- What is a possible explanation for the high rate of comorbidity between anxiety disorders and other psychological disorders?
- How do children express anxiety differently from adults?
- What are some biological explanations for why women are more likely than men to develop anxiety disorders such as agoraphobia or generalized anxiety disorder?
- How is an *ataque de nervios* similar to a panic attack? How is it different?
- Why is temporal contiguity an important concept in classical conditioning? What would happen if too much time elapsed between the presentation of the conditioned and unconditioned stimulus?
- How might the concept of stimulus generalization apply to the development of generalized anxiety disorder?
- Describe an intensive exposure technique and a gradual exposure technique. Under what circumstances might an intensive technique be preferable? When might a gradual exposure technique be more appropriate?
- What is the premise behind prolonged imaginal exposure? Why might it be useful to remember traumatic events in detail?
- How does catastrophizing or dichotomous reasoning increase one's anxiety?
- How is the flight-or-fight response involved in a panic attack?
- What is projection? How do psychodynamic theorists incorporate this defense mechanism into their explanation of a phobia?
- Explain the differences in stress hormone activity in individuals exposed to traumatic events versus individuals without trauma histories. How might such differences explain symptoms such as hypervigilance and an exaggerated startle response? Describe how this is an example of *the connection between mind and body*.

27

Multiple-Choice Questions

1. Joshua has a tendency to respond to many different situations with feelings of anxiety, as though he is in danger even when he is not. Joshua's behavior most likely reflects
   A. specific phobia
   B. state anxiety
   C. trait anxiety
   D. projection
   Ans. C

2. Aunt Sally was very embarrassed after she gave a speech at her sister's wedding—as she left the stage she tripped and fell into the wedding cake, and everyone began to laugh. Since that time, Sally is sure that she will embarrass herself in social situations and refuses to go out with friends or family, preferring instead to stay at home and watch TV. Sally most likely suffers from
   A. social phobia
   B. agoraphobia
   C. simple phobia
   D. acute stress disorder
   Ans. A

3. Which of the following anxiety disorders appears to occur at about the same rate in men and women?
   A. panic disorder
   B. OCD
   C. GAD
   D. PTSD
   Ans. B

4. Some individuals find that after having a panic attack at a neighborhood grocery store, they then fear having panic attacks in other grocery stores or even in other shopping areas. Which of the following behavioral principles best explains this phenomenon?
   A. temporal contiguity
   B. vicarious conditioning
   C. negative reinforcement
   D. stimulus generalization
   Ans. D

5. Stan has a very specific routine he goes through each day. He takes three steps forward, two steps to the side, and then one step forward each time he passes through his front door. He believes it is very important to follow this routine; if he does not, he is sure that bad luck will follow him for three weeks. Stan becomes very upset if he is rushed, and it often takes him a half-hour to leave his house. Stan's need to execute his routine is an example of
A. catastrophizing
B. contingent behavior
C. a compulsion
D. an obsession
Ans. C

6. Nancy has been having nightmares and great difficulty sleeping at night since the time of her car accident three weeks ago. She has avoided driving since the accident and finds it hard to concentrate on her work; instead she imagines the accident happening over and over again. She is also feeling jumpy and is easily startled. Nancy most likely meets the criteria for
A. post traumatic stress disorder
B. acute stress disorder
C. specific phobia
D. panic disorder
Ans. B

7. _____ is most likely to begin in childhood or adolescence, whereas _____ is rare in children.
A. Panic disorder, OCD
B. OCD, Panic disorder
C. Panic disorder, GAD
D. GAD, panic disorder
Ans. D

8. Erika's therapist has asked her to identify the least scary encounter she could have with a snake and then to progressively imagine more and more frightening situations in which she would be confronted by her worst fear—a live snake. Erika's therapist is most likely preparing to use
A. in vivo flooding
B. systematic desensitization
C. relaxation exercises
D. modeling
Ans. B

9. Tom is seeking therapy because he constantly worries about the worst-case scenario. He spends most of his time wondering how things will go wrong next and even when things seem to be going well, he feels that he is just marking time until the next terrible event occurs. When his therapist asks him to describe some fears Tom explains how even one little thing, like spilling coffee on his tie before a meeting, can ruin his whole day because he is sure no one will take him seriously. Tom's way of thinking about this situation can best be described as

A. dichotomous thinking
B. personalization
C. labeling
D. catastrophizing
Ans. D

10. _____ appears to suppress nervous system activity whereas _____ works to excite the sympathetic system.

A. GABA, norepinephrine
B. Norepinephrine, serotonin
C. Norepinephrine, GABA
D. RNCA, GABA
Ans. A

11. Mary's job is to call customers who have sent in complaints about products they have purchased. Often, when a customer is particularly rude, Mary finds herself wishing something bad would happen to make the customer have to hang up the phone. Each hour, on the hour, Mary feels she has to get up and walk around her office. If she does not walk exactly on the hour, she experiences intense anxiety. A psychodynamic theorist might offer which of the following explanations for Mary's behavior?

A. Given that Mary's sister and mother both have anxiety disorders, Mary's behavior suggests she also suffers from an anxiety disorder and that she would be aided by an SSRI.
B. Mary unconsciously believes that she can undo the effects of her anger at her customers by walking around.
C. Mary's thought distortions are causing her to personalize her customers' rudeness.
D. Mary's walking around relieves her anxiety and thus she is positively reinforced for continuing to walk each hour.
Ans. B

Short-Answer Essay Questions

1. Discuss how too much or too little anxiety can lead to abnormal behavior.

2. Compare and contrast generalized anxiety disorder (GAD) with panic disorder. Could an individual have both?

3. When does fear of a specific event or situation qualify for a diagnosis? What behaviors or emotional responses would a person have to demonstrate to meet the criteria for a specific phobia?

4. Joe is very aware of the noises his stomach makes, especially when he is anticipating a meal or just after eating. He has always felt a little embarrassed by these noises but recently they have bothered him to the point where he has stopped spending time with others before, during, or after meals. His friends are starting to complain and have asked him why he's avoiding their company. Joe does not want to offend his friends but when he hears his body making noises he is embarrassed and is sure his friends are disgusted. What diagnosis would you give Joe? Give three reasons to explain your choice.

5. Why might people living in New York City be much more likely to develop PTSD in the wake of the events of September 11, 2001, than individuals living in Boston?

6. Discuss the gender difference in anxiety disorders. What evidence is there to suggest that women have a greater biological predisposition to anxiety disorders than men? Now, discuss sociocultural explanations for higher rates of anxiety disorders in women. Which perspective do you find most compelling?

7. What is a fear hierarchy? What role does a fear hierarchy play in the application of systematic desensitization?

8. What interventions might a cognitive psychologist use to confront a client about her fear that she will be humiliated if she speaks in class? What are the potential cognitive distortions that this student likely holds?

9. Describe three types of treatment for anxiety disorders and discuss evidence of their effectiveness.

10. What is a benefit of using psychotropic medications such as tricyclic antidepressants or SSRIs to treat panic disorder? What is a disadvantage?

11. How are cognitive and behavioral approaches combined to treat a disorder such as OCD?

Chapter 6
Mood and the Mood Disorders

Learning Objectives

Defining mood and mood disorders

- Our mood fluctuates in response to the events that occur as a part of everyday life. A mood state consists not only of how we feel, but also our cognitions, motivation, and behavior. When moods are extremely low (depression) or high (mania) and seem inappropriate to the current **context** we classify them as abnormal.
- Historically, mood disorders and schizophrenia have often been confounded because both can involve hallucinations and delusions. Recently, however, experts have worked to distinguish these disorders from one another and to classify mood disorders as either unipolar (only abnormally low moods) or bipolar (alternating between abnormally high and low moods).

Classifying mood disorders

- Mood disorders are diagnosed based on the type(s) of mood episodes an individual experiences. A major depressive episode is an abnormally low mood that persists for two or more weeks and includes a combination of emotional (e.g., sadness), cognitive (e.g., difficulty concentrating), motivational (e.g., low interest), and physical (e.g., a constant feeling of fatigue) symptoms. To be diagnosed with a major depressive disorder, one must experience at least five symptoms that fall into the preceding categories.
- A major depressive episode usually lasts for at least six months if untreated. Some individuals (5–10%) experience severe depression for as long as two or more years.
- Individuals with mood disorders are at higher risk for suicide and suicide attempts. Risk varies by gender, ethnicity, and age. Caucasian males are more likely to use lethal means and complete a suicide, whereas Caucasian women have higher rates of non-lethal attempts. Individuals over the age of 75 are at greatest risk of completing a suicide. Suicide is the third leading cause of death among adolescents.
- Mania typically involves feelings that are the opposite of those experienced in depression: grandiosity, high energy, excessive talking and activity, and frenzied thoughts. In general, while depressed individuals feel lethargic, mania energizes people. To be diagnosed with a manic episode, these symptoms must cause impairment and/or distress, or psychotic symptoms must be present, and the symptoms must last at least one week.
- Manic episodes may last for several days or weeks but typically do not last as long as depressive episodes, and often they immediately precede or follow a depressive episode.
- Hypomania is a less severe form of mania—it does not impair functioning.
- To be diagnosed with a major depressive disorder, an individual must have had one or more depressive episodes, and no manic or hypomanic episodes. Bipolar I disorder is diagnosed if there has been at least one manic episode, and bipolar II disorder is diagnosed if an individual has experienced hypomanic episodes; these "highs" almost always alternate with "lows." Finally, dysthymic and cyclothymic disorders are diagnosed when mood swings are less severe but occur for at least two years.

Classification in demographic context
- Individuals seem to experience depression differently at different ages. This variation in symptoms makes it more challenging to correctly diagnose depression.
- Women are at far greater risk of developing depression than men, although no such gender difference exists for bipolar I disorder. Theorists have suggested this difference in the rate of depression may be caused by sociocultural factors such as role stress, and psychological factors such as women's greater tendency to internalize distress.
- Depression also appears to be expressed differently and occurs at varying rates in different cultures. For example, individuals in many Asian cultures are more likely to report physical symptoms such as fatigue, whereas Latinos may describe experiencing problems with their "nerves," or headaches, when they are depressed. Finally, sociocultural factors such as poverty are highly correlated with the incidence of depression.

Explaining and treating mood disorders
- Theorists have proposed genetic, neurochemical, and hormonal explanations for depression. There is clear evidence of a genetic predisposition for depression (especially severe depression within families) and bipolar disorder, based on concordance rates among twins and rates of depression among biological relatives of adoptees.
- The monoamine hypothesis suggests that in depression there may be insufficient availability of the monoamines between neurons (norepinephrine, dopamine, and serotonin) and too few receptor sites on postsynaptic neurons. Other biological theorists have noted that severely depressed individuals have excessive cortisol in their systems, perhaps as a consequence of exposure to chronic childhood stress, and suggest that this has caused permanent dysregulation in the HPA axis.
- Theorists believe that several neurotransmitters are probably involved in bipolar disorder, especially in the process of switching from one mood to another, and have noted abnormal structures in the amygdala, prefrontal cortex, and cerebellum.
- Biological interventions for mood disorders include tricyclics, MAOIs, SSRIs, and ECT for depression, and mood stabilizers such as lithium for bipolar disorder. In each case, the advantages of these interventions must be weighed against the potential adverse side effects.
- Cognitive theorists emphasize the role of cognitive distortions, particularly negative attributions about oneself, the world, and the future (the negative triad) in the development and maintenance of depression. In particular, some theorists have noted depressed individuals tend to have consistent, automatic negative thoughts such as "no one ever likes me." Cognitive therapists typically focus on helping clients identify cognitive distortions, challenging the distorted beliefs, and modifying related underlying assumptions.
- Behaviorists have noted the association between depression and decreased reinforcements and/or negative consequences for behavior. Thus, behavioral interventions are aimed at increasing reinforcements and reducing punishment on a daily basis, including helping with setting attainable goals and teaching specific life skills. Some therapists combine these techniques with cognitive restructuring. This blending of cognitive and behavioral techniques has also been effective, when combined with medication, in treating bipolar individuals.
- Psychodynamic theorists have noted the relationship between loss, anger turned inward, and feelings of inadequacy and depression. In particular, they note the risk of serious threat to self-esteem or security in childhood leading to later depression. Thus, interventions from

this perspective focus on experiences of loss, anger turned inward, traumatic childhood events, and on certain personality characteristics, such as narcissism or on overly self-critical superego.

- Sociocultural theorists note the role of gender and socioeconomic factors in depression and target interventions to address these issues. Family systems therapists address family dynamics that may facilitate a member's depression, and also focus on how a mood disorder in one member may affect other family members.
- Interpersonal therapy notes the circular relationship between mood states and relationships with others, and integrates concepts from object relational theory with cognitive and behavioral theories.

Key Terms

- Depression p. 154
- Mania p. 154
- Melancholia p. 156
- Bipolar disorders p. 156
- Unipolar disorders p. 156
- Mood episodes p. 157
- Major depressive episode p. 157
- Manic episode p. 162
- Hypomania p. 163
- Major depressive disorder p. 164
- Dysthymic disorder p. 166
- Bipolar I p. 167
- Bipolar II p. 167
- Cyclothymic p. 168
- Monoamines p.173
- Monoamine hypothesis p. 173
- Cortisol p. 173
- Tricyclics p. 174
- MOA p.174
- SSRIs p. 174
- ECT p. 176
- Lithium p. 177
- Negative cognitive triad p. 178
- Negative automatic thoughts p. 178
- Cognitive distortions p. 178
- Learned helplessness p. 179
- Pessimistic explanatory style p. 180
- Superego p. 185
- Interpersonal psychotherapy p. 188

Concept Questions

- When might we expect an extreme shift in mood? When does a mood become pathological on the *continuum between normal and abnormal behavior*?
- Why is it important to consider the *context* of an individual when we are determining whether behavior or mood is abnormal?
- When did experts distinguish unipolar mood disorders from bipolar mood disorders?
- Give an example of the different types of symptoms a depressed person might experience. Which symptoms do you think would be most debilitating?
- Why is length of time that one has experienced a mood an important consideration?
- Who is most at risk for attempting suicide? Committing suicide?
- How is hypomania different from mania? Why might someone be reluctant to seek treatment for hypomania?
- What is the difference between a major depressive episode and major depressive disorder?
- How is melancholic depression different from depression with catatonic features?
- How is postpartum depression different from the "baby blues"? What is the risk of developing the "baby blues"? Postpartum depression?
- How do criteria for childrens' mood disorders differ from adults?
- How does bipolar I differ from bipolar II? Which is more severe?
- How does depression appear in infants?
- How is depression expressed differently in different cultures?
- Describe the evidence for a genetic predisposition to depression. What other evidence is there to suggest depression may be caused by biological factors?
- What do concordance rates among individuals with bipolar suggest about the genetic heritability of this disorder?
- What is the potential link between bipolar disorder and creativity?
- What biological treatments are typically used to treat depression and bipolar disorder?
- What are some common cognitive distortions in depression?
- What is learned helplessness and how does it help us understand depression?
- What is an explanatory style? Why would a particular style make one more vulnerable to depression?
- What topics are often the focus of cognitive interventions for individuals with bipolar disorder?
- How do behaviorists explain depression? Which clients are best helped by behavioral interventions such as learning time management skills and relaxation techniques?
- What is internalization? How does Freud explain the shift from anger at another person to self-criticism?
- When might a family systems approach be useful as a treatment for depression?
- How does IPT illustrate the *principle of multiple causality*?

Multiple-Choice Questions

1. _____ and _____ were often confounded until identified as different disorders by Kraepelin in the nineteenth century.
   A. Unipolar and bipolar disorders
   B. Depression and mania
   C. Bipolar disorder and schizophrenia
   D. Unipolar depression and schizophrenia
   Ans. C

2. Sandy has been staying in bed, refusing to eat much, and feeling miserable for almost three weeks. Nothing interests her. She is not sick; she is despondent after losing her job and isn't motivated to do anything about it. Sandy is most likely experiencing
   A. a major depressive episode
   B. a manic episode
   C. a hypomanic episode
   D. a post-traumatic stress disorder
   Ans. A

3. All of the following facts about suicide are *incorrect* except
   A. The highest suicide rate is among adolescents
   B. Suicide is the third leading cause of death among teens
   C. Women are more likely to commit suicide then men
   D. African American men are at higher risk for suicide than any other ethnic group
   Ans. B

4. Hypomania is similar to mania except that
   A. it is shorter and more severe
   B. it is less severe and typically does not impair functioning
   C. it is more distressing
   D. it is harder to recover from
   Ans. B

5. Joan has felt sad for most of her life. She never really feels energetic and most of the time she would prefer to read than to spend time with others. In the past few years, Joan has found it increasingly difficult to make decisions. If Joan does have a mood disorder, which of the following disorders is most applicable?
   A. major depressive disorder
   B. hypomania
   C. dysthymic disorder
   D. cyclothymic disorder
   Ans. C

6. Kylie has been feeling great for the past week—she has been sleeping only 3 to 4 hours per night, she has been repainting her place when she gets home from work, and she has been jogging twice a day. She feels like she is at her best ever and is considering applying to graduate school (even though she did badly on her GREs) because she is sure she can write an essay that will just wow the admissions committee. Kylie's behavior best fits the criteria for
A. bipolar I disorder
B. a hypomanic episode
C. a dysthymic episode
D. cyclothymia
Ans. B

7. Research suggests that it is not only insufficient monamines in the synapses but also _____ that contributes to depression.
A. too many dendrites
B. too few action potentials
C. too few receptor sites
D. too many reuptake inhibitors
Ans. C

8. Which of the following is currently the most common biological intervention for depression?
A. SSRIs
B. Tricyclics
C. MAOIs
D. Lithium
Ans. A

9. Mike waited until later in the day to mow his lawn when it would be cooler; then a sudden storm arose, so he couldn't mow. His lawn got so long during the work week that he got a citation. He told himself, "I'm such an idiot!" In this example, Mike makes a(n) _____ attribution about why this negative event occurred.
A. external
B. internal
C. specific
D. unstable
Ans. B

10. Freud identified an overly harsh _____ as central to the development of depression.
A. id
B. ego
C. superego
D. defense mechanism
Ans. C

11. Interpersonal therapy is typically a structured, time-limited approach informed by
    A. behavioral, object-relational, and cognitive theories
    B. behavioral and humanist theories
    C. behavioral and sociocultural theories
    D. teaching specific skills and increasing rewards
    Ans. A

Short-Answer Essay Questions

1. Describe some common myths about suicide.

2. What are the criteria for a manic and a hypomanic episode? How are these mood states different from just being in a great mood?

3. What are some of the "specifiers" that may be included with a diagnosis of major depressive disorder? Why might it be important to note these particular characteristics of an individual's disorder?

4. What is seasonal affective disorder and how do we treat this disorder?

5. Discuss how the experience of depression varies by age of the individual. How does this variation affect the diagnostic process?

6. Discuss sociocultural and psychological explanations for the greater incidence of depression in women than in men.

7. Give one example each of evidence supporting genetic, neurochemical, and hormonal explanations of depression.

8. What is the most common biological intervention for bipolar disorder? What are the advantages and disadvantages of this treatment?

9. Describe the concepts of "negative cognitive triad" and "explanatory style" and discuss how these concepts relate to depression.

10. Describe a cognitive intervention for someone who has the following belief: " I am always late because I am so unorganized and incompetent. I never make a deadline or get to an appointment on time."

11. Describe the three conditions identified by Lewinsohn in his behavioral model of depression.

12. What psychodynamic topics would a therapist most likely explore with a client who is depressed?

13. Discuss at least four reasons why many individuals with bipolar disorder are noncompliant with medication.

Chapter 7
Dissociation and the Dissociative Disorders

Learning Objectives

Defining dissociation and the dissociative disorders
- Dissociation is a disruption of consciousness, memory, and/or identity.
- Dissociation can be adaptive or maladaptive depending on how functioning is affected in a given situation or **context**.
- An example of adaptive dissociation is the detachment, decreased awareness, or forgetting that sometimes facilitates someone's functioning in an emergency situation.
- An example of maladaptive functioning is when detachment, decreased awareness, or forgetting impairs a person's functioning in everyday situations.

Classifying dissociation and the dissociative disorders
- There are four dissociative disorders: depersonalization disorder, dissociative amnesia, dissociative fugue, and dissociative identity disorder.
- Depersonalization disorder is characterized by feeling detached from one's surroundings or feeling as if one is unreal.
- Dissociative amnesia, forgetting important personal information, can be generalized, selective, systematized, or continuous. Dissociative amnesia differs from organic amnesia in that it does not have a physical basis. Also, although personal information is forgotten, general informational knowledge is generally retained.
- Dissociative fugue is a rare disorder that occurs when an individual forgets his/her identity, moves to a new location, and often begins a new life as someone else.
- Dissociative identity disorder is diagnosed when an individual appears to have more than one personality or "alter" that controls his or her behavior. The different personalities may or may not know of each other and often vary in terms of age, gender, sexual orientation, and other characteristics.

Classification in demographic context
- We know little about the prevalence rates of dissociative disorders; until recently many psychologists considered these disorders to be extremely rare.
- Symptoms or signs of dissociation in adults and children are not necessarily the same.
- Currently, women are diagnosed with dissociative disorders much more frequently than men, but dissociative disorders are likely underdiagnosed in men.
- Dissociation as a phenomenon is culturally relative. In some cultures, trance states are within the range of behavior that is considered normal.

Explaining and treating dissociative disorders
- The validity of DID as a diagnosis remains a topic of debate. Proponents of the posttraumatic model argue that DID is a plausible outcome for individuals who experience severe traumatic events and develop dissociative symptoms as a form of coping. In contrast,

supporters of the sociocognitive model argue that DID exists because of media attention and cues from therapists that encourage individuals to enact multiple identities.

- Psychodynamic therapists emphasize the role of defense mechanisms such as repression, splitting, and identification in DID. These defense mechanisms are likely to be helpful at the time of the trauma, but they interfere with everyday functioning when individuals continue to rely on them.

- Behavioral theorists attend to the ways that individuals are negatively reinforced by dissociation. In other words, they suggest that someone who dissociates as a way to cope with a traumatic event experiences relief from the dissociation and is thus conditioned to dissociate again in the future. Behavioral theories have been particularly useful for designing interventions to reduce self-destructive behaviors.

- Cognitive theorists have suggested that the theories of state dependent learning and self-hypnosis offer insight into understanding dissociative disorders. They suggest that a person is most likely to recall information when in a state similar to the state in which learning occurred and that some forms of dissociation are akin to self-hypnosis. Although some cognitive theorists believe that hypnosis can be a helpful therapeutic technique, the use of hypnosis is highly controversial.

- Proponents of the biological perspective have studied drugs that can induce dissociative states to increase our understanding of the neural pathways involved in dissociation. They have noted the potential role of the thalamus in alterations of consciousness. Currently, there are no medications specifically used to treat dissociation.

- Most therapists who treat individuals with dissociative disorders, especially DID, use a multimodal approach that integrates behavioral, psychodynamic, cognitive, and biological perspectives. Some therapists use an integrated intervention strategy consisting of stages that begin with an emphasis on developing a relationship, enlisting cooperation from "alters," working to decrease dissociative episodes, exploring what individuals remember about past traumatic events and, finally, coping with and understanding these events so that the person gains an integrated sense of self.

Key Terms

- Dissociation p. 196
- Depersonalization disorder p. 198
- Dissociative amnesia p. 199
- Localized amnesia p. 199
- Selective amnesia p. 199
- Generalized amnesia p. 199
- Continuous amnesia p. 200
- Systematized amnesia p. 200
- Retrograde amnesia p. 201
- Anterograde amnesia p. 201
- Psychogenic p. 201
- Dissociative fugue p. 202
- Dissociative identity disorder p. 202
- Hysteria p. 208
- Somatoform disorders p. 208

Concept Questions

- Have you ever noticed that you arrived at your destination—class, a party, dinner at a close friend's house—with no memory of how you got there? What are other examples of normal dissociation?
- Why is dissociation frequently linked with traumatic experiences? How can dissociation act as a protective mechanism?
- When does dissociation become problematic or pathological? How does the situation or context determine what is adaptive versus maladaptive dissociation?
- Both dissociation and posttraumatic stress disorder are associated with traumatic events. How do these two disorders differ?
- Which dissociative disorder is the most common?
- If an individual develops the ability to "space out" or be "in their own world" early in life to avoid conflict or negative experiences, how can this originally adaptive behavior become problematic?
- How do systematized and selective amnesia differ?
- Is dissociative amnesia usually permanent? If not, how is dissociative amnesia typically resolved?
- What are common causes of organic amnesia?
- When someone is in a fugue state, how much do they remember about their "real" lives? How do fugue states typically end?
- Describe the different types of personalities often identified in individuals diagnosed with dissociative identity disorder.
- How is the concept of multiple personalities supported by biologically based research?
- Research with children has recently begun to describe characteristics common to children with dissociative identity disorder. In particular, some researchers have described children

with DID as having external imaginary companions. How are these personalities different from an imaginary friend that a young child who is not psychologically distressed might have?

- Why are women more likely than men to be diagnosed with dissociative disorders? Discuss at least two reasons.
- Give an example of how dissociation is defined in part by what is culturally relative for a particular group of people.
- What is the syndrome known as *amok*?
- What do the proponents of the posttraumatic model argue demonstrates the validity of DID as a diagnosis? What evidence supports the perspective of the sociocognitive model that DID is not a valid diagnosis?
- What are two possible reasons that the rate of diagnosis of DID has been increasing?
- What is selection bias? How can this phenomenon influence the results of research studies?
- How is the defense mechanism of repression related to dissociation?
- How do psychodynamic therapists work with individuals with dissociative disorders? What is the importance of a supportive stance under these circumstances?
- How did Elizabeth Loftus test her theory that memories can be reconstructed? What is a potential problem with comparing memories of being "lost" with memories of being abused?
- From the behavioral perspective, what is the role of negative reinforcement in the development of a dissociative disorder?
- The text notes a limitation to applying state dependent learning theory for individuals with dissociative disorders. Describe state dependent learning theory and discuss why an intense emotional state may adversely effect memory retrieval.
- What is an early maladaptive schema? How do cognitive therapists suggest that early memories might influence current behavior?
- What is the difference between schema compensation and schema maintenance?
- Under what circumstances is hypnosis most likely to be used? What are the concerns about using hypnosis as a therapeutic technique?
- What evidence suggests that the thalamus may be involved in dissociative processes?
- Why was sodium amytal used to help with recall of traumatic events during World War II?
- Give an example of how the behavioral, psychodynamic, and cognitive perspectives may be most useful in combination to explain dissociative disorders.
- What is the focus in Kluft's stage four: metabolism of the trauma? Why is it important to discuss the traumatic events only when the tasks identified in earlier stages are complete?

Multiple-Choice Questions

1. Sally is a 40-year-old woman who presented for therapy because she has been waking up in the morning very upset. She has dreams about her grandfather hitting her grandmother but she has no memory of this actually occurring. In fact, she realized that although she lived with her grandparents from age 5 until she was 12, she has very few memories of that time except for school events or friends' birthday parties. Which type of amnesia is Sally most likely demonstrating?
   A. organic amnesia
   B. selective amnesia
   C. continuous amnesia
   D. generalized amnesia
   Ans. B

2. Korsakoff's syndrome is a form of amnesia usually associated with
   A. systematic desensitization
   B. stroke
   C. brain injury
   D. alcoholism
   Ans. D

3. Over time Greg described three different personalities to his therapist. He explained that George is "the little guy," and that his alter Man takes care of George and hides him from Ray, while Ray tries to get Greg in trouble. Based on this brief description, which type of personality is Ray most likely to be characterized as?
   A. protective
   B. host
   C. persecutory
   D. alter
   Ans. C

4. Why are fewer men than women diagnosed with dissociative identity disorder?
   A. because men are more likely to develop schizophrenia
   B. because men are more likely to be attacked physically than sexually
   C. because men are more likely to demonstrate somatic symptoms than affective symptoms
   D. because women are more likely to seek treatment, whereas men are more likely to become involved in the legal system
   Ans. D

5. Proponents of the sociocognitive model argue the following about DID as a diagnosis:
    A. This disorder occurs as a result of cues from the media and therapists who inadvertently or purposefully reward individuals for demonstrating behaviors consistent with multiple identities.
    B. This disorder is caused by cognitive confusion related to negative social events.
    C. This diagnosis is a valid diagnosis that is useful in describing the reaction of some individuals to extremely traumatic events.
    D. That dissociation is always an adaptive response to traumatic events.
    Ans. A

6. Some studies have demonstrated that college students can act as though they have several separate identities as well as showing other signs of DID. This research supports which of the following models?
    A. postraumatic model
    B. peritraumatic model
    C. sociocognitive model
    D. social context model
    Ans. C

7. Jane works with several individuals with dissociative disorders. In her therapeutic approach, she emphasizes helping her clients to develop a clearer understanding of how traumatic events may have affected them, she focuses on developing a therapeutic alliance, and she places a greater emphasis on safety than on remembering past events. Jane is most likely working from a
    A. psychodynamic perspective
    B. cognitive perspective
    C. behavioral perspective
    D. biological perspective
    Ans. A

8. Nancy was severely abused as a child and her therapist has suggested that her expectations about how others will treat her now are influenced by these early experiences. In particular, she has suggested that Nancy's tendency to isolate herself and act as though she is not interested in relationships with others is one way that she avoids having to deal with her fears and negative emotions about these early experiences. Nancy's therapist would most likely suggest she is engaging in
    A. schema maintenance
    B. schema avoidance
    C. self-hypnosis
    D. cognitive restructuring
    Ans. B

9. Which of the following is not a drug type that has been identified as a substance which can be used to induce dissociative states?
   A. anxiolytics
   B. cannabinoids
   C. serotonergic hallucinogens
   D. NMDA receptor antagonists
   Ans. A

10. Which type of treatment is most clearly indicated in work with individuals with dissociative identity disorder?
   A. cognitive
   B. psychodynamic
   C. behavioral
   D. multimodal
   Ans. D

Short-Answer Essay Questions

1. Compare and contrast depersonalization disorder and dissociative fugue. How are these two disorders similar? How do they differ? Which do you think is more severe?

2. Which type of amnesia is usually portrayed in movies and on television? Give an example of how amnesia has been portrayed in the media. Does this example depict organic amnesia or dissociative amnesia? On what basis do psychologists distinguish between these two types of amnesia?

3. Why do you think most people with dissociative personality disorder have an "alter" that is a child? Or an "alter" that is protective of other identities?

4. Dissociation is often associated with the experience of a traumatic event. Discuss how our focus on particular types of traumatic events may skew our perception of who is most at risk for developing a dissociative disorder.

5. How does cultural *context* influence our understanding of whether trance states are adaptive or maladaptive? When do we identify trance states as pathological?

6. Discuss the two perspectives regarding the validity of DID as a diagnosis. Which perspective do you find most convincing? Why?

7. Describe how we might go about studying the frequency with which dissociation occurs. What types of biases should we work to avoid? Briefly describe some steps you would take to minimize bias in such a study.

8. Describe how a cognitive therapist and a psychodynamic therapist might approach treatment with an individual who has DID differently.

9. Describe the two perspectives in the recovered memory debate. Summarize research or evidence that supports each side of the debate. What do you think is more likely—a recovered or a reconstructed memory?

10. Describe the stages of multimodal treatment for individuals with dissociative disorders. Why do you think establishing a strong therapeutic alliance is so important? Discuss the role of the therapeutic relationship across the treatment stages.

Chapter 8
Eating, Weight, and the Eating Disorders

Learning Objectives

Defining eating disorders
- Eating disorders have gained increasing attention in recent years. Between .5% and 3% of all American women meet the criteria for anorexia nervosa, whereas 1% to 3% of women demonstrate symptoms of bulimia nervosa.
- The ***continuum between abnormal and normal behavior*** is a critical concept in this chapter, because many individuals who do not meet full criteria for an eating disorder worry excessively about their weight or engage in behaviors such as purging through vomiting. Thus, although only a small percentage of people fit the specific diagnostic criteria for an eating disorder, many people have abnormal eating behaviors or patterns.
- It is also very important to note the ***context*** of an individual with eating concerns. Many gymnasts and ballet dancers as well as fashion models maintain body weights that are well below normal. Clinicians must take into account ***context*** and decide whether the individual appears abnormal in comparison to others (e.g., among gymnasts) and also assess the mindset of the individual. For example, does he/she have the cognitive beliefs (e.g., I look fat no matter what I weigh) that are common to individuals with anorexia? Is the person likely to return to normal eating patterns once his/her surrounding circumstances change?

Classifying eating disorders
- Anorexia nervosa, bulimia nervosa, and eating disorder not otherwise specified (NOS) are the three eating disorders included in the *DSM-IV-TR*.
- To be diagnosed with anorexia, an individual must be less than 85% of normal weight for his/her height and age. He or she typically also has intense fears of gaining weight or being fat, denies the seriousness of the weight loss, and has a distorted perception of his/her body shape. In addition, body image is usually closely tied to self-evaluation. Finally, in women, there must be an absence of three or more menstrual cycles. Approximately half of those with anorexia display symptoms of depression and/or anxiety. Over time, serious physical side effects can occur, including reduced metabolism, lowered temperature and blood pressure, development of lanugo, electrolyte imbalance, as well as possible permanent damage to the skeletal and reproductive systems.
- Bulimia nervosa is diagnosed when an individual feels out of control while eating unusually large portions in a discrete period of time and then follows the binge eating with compensatory behaviors such as excessive exercise, vomiting, and laxative use. These behaviors must occur at least twice a week for three months in order to warrant the diagnosis. Finally, similar to anorexia, body image or shape is closely linked to one's self-perception. Individuals with bulimia are also prone to co-morbid mood disorders. Associated medical symptoms include: corrosion of tooth enamel, dehydration and anemia, menstrual irregularities, and electrolyte imbalances.
- Eating disorder NOS is diagnosed when individuals meet some but not all of the criteria for anorexia or bulimia and are experiencing either distress or impaired functioning.

Classification in demographic context

- Eating disordered behavior is common in females between the ages of 15 and 25. In fact, some research suggests as many as 20% of female college students have abnormal eating behaviors, and concern about eating and controlling one's eating appears in girls as young as age 8. Finally, anorexia in elderly women appears to be related to depression, fear of aging, and the wish to conform to societal standards of beauty.
- The majority of individuals with eating disorders—approximately 90%—are female. Some feminist theorists link this gender difference to societal pressures on women to be thin.
- Eating disorders are far less prevalent in less developed countries; however, as western culture exports its media, the incidence of eating disorders in other cultures has increased.
- Women of color seemed less vulnerable to the Caucasian ideals of physical beauty but more recently the incidence of eating disorders among educated, heavier African-American women has increased.
- Many people (25–60%) with abnormal eating behaviors receive the diagnosis eating disorder NOS rather than the specific diagnoses of anorexia or bulimia.
- One in three adult Americans are 20% or more over normal weight for their height, and thus they meet the definition of obesity. At this time, obesity is not a diagnosis in the *DSM-IV-TR*.

Explaining and treating eating disorders

- In general, psychodynamic theorists suggest that eating-disordered behavior is part of a complex reaction to particular family dynamics. Bruch asserted that eating disorders such as anorexia occur in individuals whose families overvalue appearance and achievement. Eating disorders are linked with control and perfectionism in studies. In addition, controlling one's body through fasting or binging and purging has been linked to sexual trauma or distress about sexual development. For example, by denying oneself food, one avoids a more adult-like, sexual figure. Interventions from the psychodynamic perspective aim to provide insight into how symptoms relate to unconscious emotional conflicts.
- Family systems theorists such as Minuchin also emphasize the role of family dynamics in the development of eating disorders. Minuchin argued that individuals develop eating disorders when their families are enmeshed. As a response to the enmeshment, the eating disorder allows the individual to be independent in the sense that she alone is in control of her body but also to be dependent in that her eating disordered behavior requires increased family involvement. However, there is little empirical evidence to support the idea that family enmeshment occurs *prior* to the onset of the eating disorder. Interventions by family therapists focus on the entire family rather than only the identified patient and often encourage the family to reach a balance between being too close and too distant from one another.
- Cognitive-behavioral theories of eating disorders focus on distorted or faulty beliefs such as equating one's self worth with one's ability to maintain a particular weight. Cognitive therapists work to identify distorted or absolute thinking about food (e.g., that it is either "good or bad") as well as reliance on rigid rules about eating that can lead to fasting or binging. Often, clients are asked to self-monitor or record their food-related thoughts and behaviors so that therapists can help them identify distortions related to eating.
- Sociocultural theorists suggest that because the media has increasingly represented thin, beautiful women as successful, popular and powerful, many women strive to meet these

unrealistic standards of beauty. In addition, they argue that individuals who do not meet these standards believe that they are lazy, unattractive, and lacking in self-control. Sociocultural theorists rely on education to prevent eating disorders and employ social activism in an attempt to change how women are represented in the media.

- Biological theorists focus on genetics and the role of certain hormones and neurotransmitters in eating disorders. There are higher concordance rates for anorexia and bulimia in identical twins than in fraternal twins. There are also differences in hormone and neurotransmitter levels, but it is unclear whether these differences are the cause or result of eating disorders. Research indicates that SSRIs combined with CBT are an effective means of treating bulimia. Relatively few studies have been done on SSRIs and anorexia, but preliminary results suggest SSRIs may be useful in conjunction with therapy to prevent relapse.

Key Terms

- Anorexia nervosa p. 228
- Electrolytes p. 229
- Restricting type anorexia p. 230
- Binge-eating/purging type anorexia p. 230
- Bulimia nervosa p. 230
- Purging type bulimia p. 232
- Nonpurging type bulimia p. 232
- Eating disorder not otherwise specified p. 232
- Subclinical p. 234
- Reverse anorexia p. 235
- Obesity p. 238
- Enmeshed p. 241
- Identified patient p. 242
- Catastrophizing p. 246
- Endorphins p. 249
- SSRI p. 249

Concept Questions

- How do we determine when eating patterns are abnormal?
- What are the primary differences between anorexia and bulimia?
- What are common side effects of anorexia and bulimia?
- What are common co-morbid diagnoses for individuals with bulimia?
- When should we consider using the diagnosis eating disorder NOS?
- What are common standards of beauty for men and women? How do these ideals influence the different kinds of disorders expressed primarily by women and by men?
- What is the feminist argument for how standards of beauty serve to prevent women from increasing their social power?
- What do we know about eating disorders and abnormal eating patterns in females at different ages?

- What is the prevalence of eating disorders in different cultures? In industrialized societies versus less developed cultures?
- What did Becker and her colleagues find when they studied girls in Fiji before and after exposure to western media? Did these results surprise you? Why or why not?
- How well do current eating disorder diagnoses capture individuals' abnormal patterns of eating?
- How do we define obesity? Why do you think it is *not* currently included in the *DSM-IV-TR*? Do you think it should be?
- How do psychodynamic theorists explain eating disorders? How is this explanation similar to one that might be offered by a family systems theorist?
- Who is the "identified patient" and why is this concept important in family therapy?
- How could we test the extent to which enmeshed family relationships cause versus maintain eating disorders? Why do we make this distinction?
- What is catastrophizing and how is it related to disordered eating?
- How might cognitive therapists attempt to help clients understand their distorted beliefs about eating? What steps would a cognitive therapist take to challenge faulty beliefs?
- How do sociocultural theorists explain eating disorders? What do they think will change or prevent the rates of eating disorders?
- What evidence supports the biological perspective on eating disorders?
- According to empirical research, what types of treatment are most effective in treating bulimia?
- Describe the ***connection between mind and body*** in eating disorders? How does starvation affect the body? The mind?

Multiple-Choice Questions

1. A side effect of _____ can be an imbalance of electrolytes.
   A. anorexia nervosa
   B. bulimia nervosa
   C. anorexia nervosa and bulimia nervosa
   D. borderline personality disorder
   Ans. C

2. Suzy's behavior has changed dramatically over the past six months. On several occasions, she has refused to eat more than a few carrots or a small bowl of applesauce and some dry toast for an entire day; her friends are very worried, but she does not seem to be losing any weight. Suzy's roommate Carla also has noticed that food has been disappearing from their kitchen, including two bags of chips and a gallon of ice cream in just the past day. Based on this limited description, Suzy most likely has
   A. restricting type anorexia
   B. binge eating/purging type anorexia
   C. purging type bulimia
   D. nonpurging type bulimia
   Ans. D

3. If an individual routinely engages in bouts of eating that seem out of his or her control and also has a negative self-perception but does not use any compensatory behaviors, he or she most likely would be diagnosed with _____.
   A. eating disorder NOS
   B. binge eating/purging type anorexia
   C. purging type bulimia
   D. nonpurging type bulimia
   Ans. A

4. Research suggests that many females demonstrate concerns about weight and monitor their food intake
   A. when menstruation and hormonal cycles begin
   B. by age 8 or 9
   C. starting in high school
   D. by age 5
   Ans. B

5. A condition found primarily in men that involves excessive worry about not being muscular enough and underdeveloped is called _____.
   A. opposite anorexia
   B. eating disorder NOS
   C. reverse anorexia
   D. reverse bulimia
   Ans. C

6. Research on girls' exposure to TV shows such as "Beverly Hills 90210" and "ER" in a cultural group previously unfamiliar with western media indicated that
   A. girls are not affected by television as much as by family values about healthy eating
   B. the majority of the girls' behavior or self-image changed dramatically over the course of just a few years of exposure to western ideals of beauty
   C. some girls' behavior may change but the majority do not express concerns about their weight or appearance
   D. only those girls who watched "90210" showed disordered eating
   Ans. B

7. Family systems theorists are most likely to argue that
   A. eating disorders are caused by parents who emphasize appearance and achievement
   B. eating disorders are caused by enmeshed, overinvolved parents
   C. eating disorders are caused and maintained by enmeshed boundaries
   D. given the lack of empirical evidence that enmeshed boundaries cause eating disorders, at this point it is most reasonable to assert that eating disorders appear to be maintained by enmeshed boundaries
   Ans. D

8. The explanation that individuals engage in abnormal eating because of ideas like "I am a failure if I can't even control how much I eat" best represents a
    A. cognitive perspective
    B. psychodynamic perspective
    C. family systems perspective
    D. biological perspective
    Ans. A

9. Tara thinks that "if I eat a slice of pizza, I'll turn into a complete pig and eat so much everyone else will be grossed out so I won't have any at all." This is an example of
    A. selective abstraction
    B. circular thinking
    C. dichotomous reasoning
    D. triangular thinking
    Ans. C

10. Research suggests that _____ is the most effective treatment for bulimia.
    A. CBT
    B. SSRIs
    C. the combination of CBT and SSRIs
    D. ABC therapy
    Ans. C

Short-Answer Essay Questions

1. What are common psychological and medical side effects of anorexia?

2. How is self-perception involved in the development and maintenance of an eating disorder?

3. Elaine has been very thin for two years. For several months she did not menstruate and felt that she was fat, even though her weight was about 80% of normal body weight for her height. She describes having gone through a period when she did not allow herself to eat anything except for a bowl of raisins, yogurt, and cereal daily. In the past 6 months, however, she has slowly gained weight and is eating more regularly—she reports eating three small meals per day. However, she is fearful of impulses that seem beyond her control. Just two days ago, Elaine described eating a bucket of fried chicken, two servings of mashed potatoes, and two sides of pasta salad in one sitting and then forcing herself to throw up. Although she felt quite ill, she has had an urge to eat a large amount of food again today. Discuss how Elaine met or meets the criteria for various eating disorders and how her experience demonstrates the fluidity of these disorders.

4. How does the spread of eating disorders across cultures support a sociocultural explanation of eating disorders? Discuss Becker and colleagues' Fiji study to support your response.

5. How is socioeconomic status associated with eating disorders?

6. Compare and contrast how a family systems therapist and cognitive-behavioral therapist might approach treating an individual with anorexia.

7. Discuss feminist perspectives (such as arguments by Faludi and Wolf) on eating disorders. Do you agree or disagree with these arguments? State your reasoning.

8. How does the principle of *multiple causality* inform our treatment approach to eating disorders? If you could combine any of the available interventions or approaches, what do you think would be an ideal treatment approach? Discuss your reasoning.

Chapter 9
Drug Use and Substance Use Disorders

Learning Objectives

Defining drug use and substance use disorders
- Approximately 25% of the U.S. population will meet the criteria for a substance use disorder during their lifetime. Drug use, especially alcohol and nicotine, are linked with a quarter of all deaths in this country.
- Drugs are not necessarily illegal; rather, a drug is any psychoactive or brain-affecting substance. Drug use is common in daily life across cultures. People use substances or drugs regularly to obtain a feeling of pleasure or to decrease stress or tension.
- Looking at drug use in *context* is one way that clinicians assess whether drug use is pathological. Thus, rather than simply determining how much of a drug a person is using, a clinician explores the relationship between the person and the substance, assessing the extent to which using the substance causes harm or distress and impairs his/her functioning.

Classifying substance use disorders
- Substance abuse is diagnosed when there is continued use of a substance despite adverse consequences, such as impaired functioning at work/school/home or in interpersonal relationships, drug use in dangerous situations, and/or involvement in drug-related legal problems. This diagnosis does not require any physiological dependence on the drug or evidence of tolerance or withdrawal symptoms.
- Substance dependence is diagnosed when there is continued use after adverse outcomes, plus patterns of compulsive use and loss of control regarding use. Dependence often involves drug tolerance and/or withdrawal symptoms as well.

Commonly abused substances
- Most drugs can be classified as either depressants, stimulants, or hallucinogens.
- Barbiturates, Methaqualone (Quaalude), opioids, Benzodiazepines (Valium, Xanax) and alcohol are depressants that slow down the central nervous system (CNS). Alcohol is the most commonly abused substance in the United States. Alcoholism is a commonly used term for alcohol dependence. Opioids are substances derived from the opium poppy such as heroin, Vicodin, and Demoral. These substances work to depress the CNS and, in addition, bind to opioid sites throughout the body; they are powerful suppressants of pain and produce a feeling of euphoria and sedation.
- Stimulants work to increase CNS activity. Individuals who take these drugs usually feel more alert and energetic. Cocaine, amphetamines, methylphenidate (Ritalin), and nicotine are all stimulants. Stimulants are used to treat medical conditions such as asthma or urinary incontinence as well as to treat disorders such as attention deficit hyperactivity disorder. Stimulants such as amphetamines are frequently used to aid in weight loss but are controversial because the weight loss is often temporary and there are often negative side effects. Nicotine, owing to its usual method of delivery–smoking–is currently the deadliest drug in existence throughout the world. Although nicotine use is decreasing in the United

States, tobacco companies have been targeting overseas markets and smoking has increased in many countries. Low to moderate amounts of caffeine are not usually considered a health risk. However, high levels of caffeine have been associated with some negative outcomes.

- Hallucinogens are substances that produce sensory perceptions which are not based on external stimuli but rather are generated internally. Hallucinogens have been used for many centuries, sometimes in spiritual ceremonies and practices. LSD, a synthetic hallucinogen drugs causes profound perceptual changes, depersonalization, and enhanced emotionality.
- Other drugs such as marijuana, Ecstasy, PCP, GHB, and steroids do not fit neatly into the three preceding categories of drugs but are commonly used and abused.

Explaining and treating substance use disorders

- Historically, explanations of substance misuse have typically been presented either from the disease model perspective or the legal/moral perspective. For example, during colonial times, people who drank alcohol to excess were viewed as morally lacking or having a bad character. A third view, a psychological perspective, argues that substance misuse is a symptom caused by other underlying problems such as emotional distress. Currently, the disease model predominates.
- The biological perspective emphasizes the reinforcing effects of drugs through the dopamine system as well as genetic factors in addiction. Biological interventions consist of medications designed to cause adverse reactions if combined with the substance to be avoided, substitution therapies, and medications aimed at reducing cravings.
- Sociocultural theorists note the high correlations between social variables such as poverty or unemployment and substance misuse. In general, they note the important role of the *context* or circumstances in drug use. Many individuals begin substance use under stressful conditions such as war, work pressures, or when encouraged by peer groups. Thus, sociocultural interventions include generating social support from friends and family. Similarly, family systems theorists note the role of family members in "enabling" the substance misuse and work to challenge these patterns of interaction within the family.
- Behavioral theorists emphasize the ability of drugs to reduce tension or distress and thus the reinforcement an individual receives from using substances. Cognitive theorists note the role of beliefs and expectations involved in substance misuse. Interventions from these perspectives includes techniques such as cognitive restructuring, covert sensitization, contingency management, and aversion therapies.
- Psychodynamic theorists regard substance misuse as a symptom related to underlying problems or emotional conflicts. These theorists also emphasize the role of the defense mechanism of denial in substance misuse. Psychodynamic interventions are usually adjunctive to other treatments in the case of severe substance use problems, but generally aim to improve a person's self-esteem and relationships in order to decrease the individual's need to self-medicate with drugs.
- Twelve-step programs are self-help groups with a spiritual emphasis that advocate complete abstinence and offer a sponsor to help support the individual's attempt to stay sober.

Key Terms

- Binge drinking p. 256
- Denial p. 256
- Substance abuse p. 260
- Substance dependence p. 261
- Tolerance p. 261
- Withdrawal p. 261
- Polysubstance abuse p. 264
- Dual diagnosis p. 264
- Depressants p. 266
- Alcoholism p. 266
- Fetal alcohol syndrome p. 269
- Sedatives p. 269
- Hypnotics p. 269
- Anxiolytic p. 269
- Cross-tolerance p. 270
- Synergistic p. 271
- Opioids p. 271
- Narcotics p. 272
- Analgesia p. 272
- Endogenous p. 272
- Endorphins p. 272
- Stimulants p. 272
- Cocaine p. 273
- Amphetamines p. 274
- Caffeine p. 276
- Hallucinogens p. 277
- LSD p. 279
- Psilocybin p. 281
- Peyote p. 281
- Mescaline p. 281
- Marijuana p. 282
- Half-life p. 282
- Ecstasy p. 283
- PCP p. 283
- Ketamine p. 283
- GHB p. 284
- Inhalants p. 284
- Anabolic steroids p. 284
- Self-medication p. 287
- Flipped switch theory p. 289
- Substitution (or maintenance) therapy p. 290
- Network therapy p. 292
- Codependency p. 292
- Identified patient p. 292

Concept Questions

- What is binge drinking?
- How do clinicians draw the line between normal and abnormal substance use? To what extent do they rely on quantitative factors? What else can they use to identify pathological use of drugs?
- Which depressant is the most commonly abused substance in the United States? Why do you think this drug is more abused than others?
- How does alcohol affect the central nervous system?
- Why is gender important to consider when evaluating the impact of alcohol on an individual?
- What is fetal alcohol syndrome?
- What are the dangers of sedatives and hypnotics?
- Why might a benzodiazepine be used to treat alcohol dependence?
- What is a synergistic effect? Do you think this effect is well understood by the general public?
- What did the manufacturer of Rohypnol do to prevent its use as a date rape drug? How do people get access to this drug?
- What are narcotics? What are the main effects of these substances?
- What is the process by which endorphins are released? Do you think people can become addicted to endorphins? Why or why not?
- Describe the withdrawal symptoms in opiate addiction.
- What are some medical uses for stimulants?
- What are the possible methods of administration for cocaine?
- How do clinicians treat cocaine addiction?
- How do amphetamines work in the CNS? What neurotransmitters do they affect?
- How does nicotine enter the body and what are its effects?
- What are the effects of caffeine at moderate and at high doses?
- How do hallucinogens affect individuals who ingest them? Why were hallucinogens made illegal in the United States?
- Why do you think marijuana is the most widely used illegal drug?
- What are the common effects of marijuana? What are some long-term effects of regular use?
- What are potential risks of using Ecstasy?
- Why do many experts disagree with classifying PCP as a hallucinogen?

- How does PCP affect pain tolerance?
- What is GHB?
- Who is most likely to use inhalants?
- What are legitimate uses of anabolic steroids?
- What is the actual effect of an anabolic steroid on performance? What explanation do we have for changes in performance by users of anabolic steroids?
- What is the "disease model" of addiction?
- What are the advantages and disadvantages of relying on the disease model as an explanation of substance misuse?
- What is the evidence for genetic factors contributing to alcoholism?
- What is the "flipped switch" theory?
- Why do family therapists avoid focusing on the "identified patient?" What other patterns or behaviors are they working to identify?
- What is the "tension reduction" motive for substance use?
- What is alexithymia?
- Why do psychodynamic theorists emphasize the role of denial in substance disorders?
- What is "self-medication" from a psychodynamic perspective?
- What is a" twelve-step" group and how effective is this form of treatment compared with others?

Multiple-Choice Questions

1. In general, clinicians have shifted from relying on a quantitative definition of abnormal drug use to
   A. working to understand the context in which drugs are used and the extent to which this causes an individual distress and/or impairment
   B. assessing how much substance is ingested daily
   C. understanding how drugs affect neurotransmitter levels in the brain and using this to define abuse
   D. employing legal definitions of abuse so that they are in agreement with the courts
   Ans. A

2. The primary difference between substance abuse and substance dependence is
   A. that substance abuse is more likely to lead to legal problems
   B. that someone can abuse a substance without being dependent on it
   C. that substance abuse results from loss of control, whereas dependence is based on continued use despite adverse consequences
   D. that substance abuse is diagnosed after someone has one problem but dependence is based on a pattern
   Ans. B

3. Which of the following statements is false?
   A. Marijuana has very low potential for physical addiction but is associated with paranoia and a psychotic-like state at very high doses.
   B. Marijuana is typically smoked and has moderate potential for psychological addition.
   C. Marijuana is highly physically addictive.
   D. Marijuana is a drug to which individuals can develop a tolerance and thus must use more to get the same effect.
   Ans. C

4. Which of the following currently has no common medical uses?
   A. stimulants
   B. opiates
   C. steroids
   D. hallucinogens
   Ans. D

5. Which of the following is a substance used to cause disinhibition and loss of memory and is referred to as a "date rape" drug?
   A. Xanax
   B. Rohypnol
   C. Amytal
   D. Percodan
   Ans. B

6. Withdrawal symptoms for _____ are generally extremely uncomfortable and include flulike symptoms—tremors, chills, sweating, and cramps.
   A. LSD
   B. cocaine
   C. heroin
   D. marijuana
   Ans. C

7. _____ is sometimes combined with _____ ; this combination is known as a "speedball" and is used to lessen the effects of withdrawal.
   A. Cocaine, heroin
   B. Opium, benzodiazepines
   C. Cocaine, benzodiazepines
   D. Heroin, rohypnol
   Ans. A

8. Which of the following drugs is associated with the greatest number of deaths?
   A. cocaine
   B. methamphetamine
   C. heroin
   D. nicotine
   Ans. D

9. According to your text, _____ have been used as a part of spiritual practice for many centuries.
   A. stimulants
   B. hallucinogens
   C. depressants
   D. opiates
   Ans. B

10. The long "half-life" of marijuana is related to
    A. the length of time that one is "high" after smoking or ingesting marijuana
    B. the amount of time it takes for the leaves to dry and ready to be used for smoking
    C. the experience of regular users becoming "chronically" stoned
    D. the amount of THC relative to DST
    Ans. C

11. Although Ecstasy is often used because it induces pleasurable feelings and a sense of connection with others, it also has been linked with deaths due to _____.
    A. dehydration and hyperthermia
    B. increased heart rate
    C. sedation and depressed CNS
    D. tremors and eventual stroke in cases of an overdose
    Ans. A

12. The _____ model argues that alcohol is addictive and abstinence is the only cure.
    A. moral
    B. legal
    C. disease
    D. symptom
    Ans. C

13. Which of the following is the most compelling evidence for a strong genetic component in substance misuse?
    A. 25% of the sons of alcoholics become alcoholic themselves
    B. there are structural similarities in the brains of fathers and sons who are both alcoholic
    C. changes in neurotransmitter levels occur in alcoholics and in their children who drink
    D. adopted boys whose biological parent(s) were alcoholics are three to four times more likely to be alcoholics than adopted sons whose biological parents were not alcoholic
    Ans. D

14. _____ is the method of treatment that uses a safer substitute substance to prevent relapse.
    A. Maintenance therapy
    B. Disulfiram therapy
    C. Twelve-step therapy
    D. Controlled use therapy
    Ans. A

15. Alexis is furious because her husband is drinking again. She hates it when he drinks because it affects their social life. For example, they have to leave gatherings with friends early—before his behavior gets outrageous. She also ends up having to take care of everything—paying all their bills and making sure there are groceries in the house. A family therapist would probably suggest to Alexis that
    A. she should take her husband to rehab and get him on Antabuse
    B. he will probably always be a problem drinker because he has stressful job and serious financial concerns
    C. she "enables" his drinking because she takes responsibility for everything rather than allowing him to deal with the consequences of his drinking
    D. she should reward her boyfriend each time he avoids drinking and refuse to socialize with him if he does drink
    Ans. C

Short-Answer Essay Questions

1. Describe the difference between a diagnosis of substance abuse and substance dependence.

2. What are potential physical and social long-term effects of alcohol dependence?

3. What are the medical uses of drugs such as benzodiazepines, morphine, and methadone? What are the risks of using these drugs?

4. What are the most common medical uses of amphetamines? Why are some of these uses controversial?

5. What are the known consequences of using nicotine? Why do you think so many people continue to smoke given the harmful effects of nicotine?

6. How did researchers learn about the effects of LSD? What are the ethical concerns regarding experimentation with this drug by the agencies of the U.S. government?

7. Why do substances such as GHB, Rohypnol, and Ketamine have the potential to be used as "date rape" drugs? What are the effects of these drugs?

8. Describe three different exploratory theoretical perspectives on substance misuse.

9. How does social learning theory suggest that individuals develop addictions? What prevention methods do we use to counteract social learning that encourages addictive behaviors?

10. Compare and contrast the behavioral and cognitive perspectives on substance misuse.

11. How do psychodynamic theorists explain substance misuse? How does this differ from the disease model?

Chapter 10
Sex, Gender, and the Sexual Disorders

Learning Objectives

Defining sexual disorders
- Sexuality and sexual behaviors are a normal part of life for most people. However, because some aspects of sexuality can be confusing and emotionally intense, many people are conflicted when faced with issues concerning their sexual choices and behaviors.
- The line between abnormal and normal sexuality is not clear. The **context** in which sexual behaviors take place is relevant to deciding when behaviors are abnormal; however, our definitions of sexual abnormality are not precise, and **historical and cultural relativism** affect these definitions.

Classifying sexual disorders
- Sexual dysfunctions are persistent problems during three of the four phases of sexual response: sexual interest, arousal, and orgasm. The fourth phase, resolution, has no dysfunctions associated with it. To be classified as a sexual dysfunction, a problem must occur on a consistent basis and cause distress and/or interpersonal problems. Sexual dysfunctions may be caused by lack of information or sexual experience, performance anxiety, medical problems, or emotions such as shame or guilt related to sexual behavior. Treatments such as sensate focus aim to reduce pressure for specific results (e.g., orgasm) and to increase sexual pleasure and general sensual awareness.
- Sexual desire dysfunctions include hypoactive sexual desire (lack of desire), and sexual aversion, an extreme avoidance of sexual contact. Arousal dysfunctions include female sexual arousal disorder and male erectile disorder. Female and male orgasmic disorders consist of an inability to reach, or a long delay before reaching, orgasm following normal arousal. Premature ejaculation is also grouped with the orgasm dysfunctions. In addition to the preceding dysfunctions, some individuals experience pain associated with intercourse, classified as either vaginismus or dyspareunia.
- Most dysfunctions can be effectively treated with therapy or medication.
- Paraphilias, formerly known as perversions, are far less common than sexual dysfunctions but much more severe. A paraphilia is a pattern of abnormal sexual arousal and preference, such as for a nonhuman object, or a nonconsenting sexual relationship. Many sexual practices related to the paraphilias, such as voyeurism, are not considered pathological if they are carried out in moderation and with mutual consent. In other words, they fall along the **continuum between normal and abnormal behavior**. However, when the practices are persistent and necessary for sexual arousal and when they cause distress or impairment, they are considered abnormal.
- Rape is not included as a paraphilia in the *DSM-IV-TR* even though it might seem to fit the diagnosis of sexual sadism. One reason for this is the argument that rape results from hostile tendencies rather than deviant sexual arousal.

Diagnoses: Paraphilias

- Exhibitionism, voyeurism, fetishism, sexual sadism, sexual masochism, pedophilia, and frotteurism are the most common forms of paraphilia listed in the *DSM-IV-TR*. Exhibitionists expose themselves to unsuspecting others and most exhibitionists report that their intent is to humiliate, shock, and/or arouse women who are strangers. Voyeurs watch individuals in the process of disrobing or engaging in sexual behaviors without their consent. Individuals with fetishism experience arousal in response to inanimate objects. Transvestism is a form of fetishism involving a preference to wear women's clothing for purposes of arousal. Sexual sadism is diagnosed when causing another pain is necessary for sexual arousal. (This is distinct from the normal tendency of many people to consensually enjoy some mild aggression during sexual interactions.) Pedophilia is a paraphilia in which children are used for sexual gratification. Current research suggests that between 10 to 20% of youths in the United States experience some form of sexual abuse by the age of 18. Although the majority of pedophiles are men, a significant percentage are female. Frotteurism is the practice of rubbing against a stranger for sexual gratification.

Explaining and treating the paraphilias

- Recent psychodynamic explanations of paraphilias suggest that they involve a particular form of hostility, specifically an unconscious attempt to humiliate someone as retribution for humiliation the individual experienced as a child. Early psychodynamic explanations had focused more on fixations in sexual development.
- Cognitive behavioral theorists emphasize the role of social learning and classical conditioning in paraphilias.
- The biological perspective emphasizes that injuries to different parts of the brain and/or illness can be associated with paraphilias.
- Treatment of individuals with paraphilias is usually very difficult. Most individuals with these disorders do not seek treatment on their own and are not motivated to change. In addition, clinicians can have negative reactions to these individuals and thus counter-transference can interfere with a good working alliance between the clinician and client.

Gender identity disorders

- Gender identity disorder is diagnosed when an individual's gender (psychological sense of being male or female) is not the same as his/her biological sex (physical body), and the individual feels very uncomfortable with their biological sex. This disorder is very rare, but it is more common in men than in women. Generally, GID is diagnosed in childhood, and most people so diagnosed eventually identify as gay, lesbian, or bisexual when they become adults.
- The causes of GID are not clear. Biological theorist have suggested that exposure to prenatal, postnatal, or even pubertal hormones may contribute to GID; however, research has not provided any conclusive evidence for this. Psychodynamic theorists have suggested that a disturbed mother–son relationship may lead to GID, research suggests mothers of boys with GID are more likely to have been withdrawn and depressed than overly gratifying and intrusive. Behaviorists argue that cross-gender behaviors in GID must have been strongly reinforced. Finally, family systems and sociocultural theorists have noted that social reinforcement for cross-gender behaviors outside the family; being one of many siblings; being much younger than siblings; significant family stress and pathology; and

difficulties with limit setting are all associated with GID. In general, the ***principle of multiple causality*** helps us to understand that integrating these different perspectives offers the best explanation of the development of gender identity disorder.

- Treatment of GID in childhood is controversial. Some clinicians argue that treatment is essential, because children are experiencing great distress. However, other clinicians argue that such interventions are aimed at preventing homosexuality and are unethical. Treatment for adults with GID includes the possibility of sex reassignment, but this is a long, stressful, and expensive process, and the long-term consequences of these procedures are not yet known.

Key Terms

- Ego-dystonic homosexuality p. 310
- Sexual dysfunctions p. 315
- Paraphilias p. 315
- Hypoactive sexual desire p. 317
- Sexual aversion p. 318
- Female sexual arousal disorder p. 319
- Male erectile disorder p. 319
- Female orgasmic disorder p. 320
- Male orgasmic disorder p. 320
- Premature ejaculation p. 320
- Vaginismus p. 321
- Dyspareunia p. 321
- Exhibitionism p. 324
- Voyeurism p. 324
- Fetishism p. 325
- Transvestic fetishism p. 326
- Sexual sadism p. 326
- Sexual masochism p. 328
- Pedophilia p. 328
- Frotteurism p. 328
- Turning passive into active p. 332
- Countertransference p. 334
- Phallometric assessment p. 335
- Masturbatory satiation p. 335
- Chemical castration p. 336
- Gender identity disorder p. 336
- Gender p. 336
- Temperament p. 342
- Sex change p. 344

Concept Questions

- When is sexual behavior considered pathological?
- What is the distinction between sexual dysfunctions and paraphilias?
- Describe the sexual response cycle.
- What are some interventions used to assist individuals or couples with sexual dysfunctions?
- What is the difference between hypoactive sexual desire and sexual aversion?
- What is the most common intervention for erectile disorder?
- What is female orgasmic disorder? How common is it?
- What is the "squeeze technique" and what is it used for?
- What are common causes of painful intercourse?
- What are some demographic characteristics of individual with paraphilias?
- What do most exhibitionists indicate is their reason for exposing themselves? To whom do they prefer to expose themselves?
- How does voyeurism differ from enjoying watching a movie with sexually explicit scenes?
- When is sexual arousal in response to an inanimate object fetishism? When is it normal?
- How does transvestism differ from cross-dressing due to gender dysphoria?
- How does the author of "Unlikely Obsession" explain her desire to be spanked? Does her explanation make sense to you? Why or why not?
- What are common current treatment techniques for individuals with paraphilias?
- What is GID?
- What outcomes are common for individuals diagnosed with GID in childhood?
- What are some interventions used with children diagnosed with GID?

Multiple-Choice Questions

1. Which of the following can cause a sexual dysfunction?
   A. performance anxiety
   B. sexual inexperience
   C. lack of information about sex
   D. all of the above
   Ans. D

2. Clara is very distressed because her sexual problems are affecting her marriage. She reports that she likes the idea of having intercourse with her husband but states she never fantasizes about him or becomes aroused when he tries to initiate sexual interactions. Clara most likely is struggling with
   A. sexual aversion disorder
   B. hypoactive sexual desire
   C. female orgasmic disorder
   D. dyspareunia
   Ans. B

3. Exhibitionists typically give which of the following reasons for exposing themselves to women?
   A. they are too shy to initiate any kind of relationship with women they know
   B. they have severe performance anxiety and can feel aroused only when the other person has no expectations
   C. they want to shock the observer
   D. they hope that the observer will shun them
   Ans. C

4. Sexual arousal that always requires the presence of a specific inanimate object is
   A. normal
   B. fetishism
   C. voyeurism
   D. exhibitionism
   Ans. B

5. The majority of boys diagnosed with GID
   A. engage in transvestism as adults
   B. identify as gay or bisexual by adulthood and no longer express gender dysphoria
   C. pursue sex reassignment
   D. become heterosexual adults without gender dysphoria
   Ans. B

Short-Answer Essay Questions

1. Discuss changing views on masturbation and homosexuality, using the core concept of historical relativism.

2. Describe two types of sexual dysfunctions and give an example of how each dysfunction might be treated.

3. What is the definition of a paraphilia? Why is rape not included as a paraphilia?

4. Describe three paraphilias, and the demographic characteristics of individuals with paraphilias.

5. What is sexual sadism? When is aggressive sexual behavior "normal?"

6. Why is treatment of individuals with paraphilias often difficult?

7. What are possible reasons for the greater prevalence of gender identity disorder in males than in females?

8. Why is treating GID in children controversial? Describe behavioral and psychodynamic interventions for GID in children, and discuss whether you agree or disagree with the use of these treatment approaches.

Chapter 11
Personality and the Personality Disorders

Learning Objectives

Defining personality and the personality disorders
- Personality traits are characteristics that are generally consistent across time and situations. Personality disorders are diagnosed on the basis of maladaptive, rigid, and extreme traits. These traits typically begin by late adolescence or early adulthood, are stable over time, and are not normal within the individual's cultural *context*. In addition, the traits lead to impairment or distress.
- Many of the traits associated with personality disorders are exaggerated versions of normal traits. Personality disorders exist at the extreme end of the continuum between normal and abnormal personality traits.

Classifying, explaining, and treating the personality disorders
- **Cluster A**, the odd or eccentric personality disorders, consists of the paranoid, schizoid, and schizotypal personality disorders.
  - Individuals with paranoid personality disorder are distrustful and overly suspicious of others. The suspicions must be either unwarranted or exaggerated given the individual's circumstances. The prevalence of this disorder is approximately .5 to 2.5% of the population.
  - Cognitive-behavioral perspectives on personality disorders emphasize the role of childhood experiences in shaping how individuals understand and interpret their world. These theorists focus on assumptions, beliefs, and interpersonal strategies that support paranoid traits in their interventions with individuals with paranoid personality disorder.
  - Psychodynamic theorists suggest that personality disorders involve maladaptive defense mechanisms that develop in response to repetitive, negative childhood experiences. These theorists propose that paranoid personality disorder develops when individuals experience chronic humiliation and ridicule in childhood and learned to "attack" others before being attacked. They also assert that the expectation of attack from others is due in part to projection, the defense mechanism in which one's own hostile feelings are attributed to another.
  - Schizoid personality disorder is diagnosed when an individual lacks interest in relationships and displays a limited range of emotions. People with this diagnosis often appear indifferent to others—even family members or significant others. This disorder is rare, with a prevalence of .8%.
  - Biological theorists have noted the important role of temperament in the development of some personality disorders. For example, these theorists hypothesize that infants and toddlers with sensitive temperaments who are easily over stimulated and who have active or intrusive caregivers learn to withdraw from interactions to protect themselves and thus develop personality traits associated with schizoid and schizotypal personality disorders. Psychodynamic theorists also emphasize

withdrawal from others in their explanation of schizoid personality disorder; however, they relate this pattern of disengagement to problems in early attachment. In addition, these theorists focus on the defense mechanism of intellectualization in schizoid personality disorder.

- o Schizotypal personality disorder consists of a pattern of eccentric or odd behavior, distorted beliefs, and discomfort in interpersonal relationships. Some theorists have argued that the extent of eccentric thoughts and behaviors in these individuals suggests that this disorder may in fact be a mild form of schizophrenia; however, individuals with schizotypal personality disorder are not as severely out of touch with reality as are those with schizophrenia. Examples of strange beliefs held by individuals with schizotypal personality disorder include ideas of reference and magical thinking.
- o Biological theorists have noted similar structural and neurotransmitter abnormalities in the brains of individuals with schizotypal personality disorder and schizophrenia.
- **Cluster B,** the dramatic, emotional, or erratic personality disorders, consists of antisocial, borderline, histrionic, and narcissistic personality disorder.
  - o Generally, a person with antisocial personality disorder shows a consistent, longstanding disregard for and willingness to violate the rights of others that begins in childhood or adolescence and continues into adulthood. There is a prevalence rate of 2% for this disorder. Although, these individuals may be criminals, they do not have to be in legal trouble to meet the criteria for antisocial personality disorder. Instead, the primary characteristic for this disorder is a lack of empathy or concern about how one's actions will affect others.
  - o The *principle of multiple causality* is central to explaining antisocial personality disorder, because it seems best described by a combination of biological, psychodynamic, cognitive, and sociocultural concepts. Biological theorists have noted the low levels of anxiety demonstrated by individuals with antisocial personality disorder when they engage in tasks that typically produce high levels of anxiety in most people. There is also evidence that some individuals with antisocial personality disorder may have been exposed to drugs such as cocaine, nicotine, or marijuana in utero. However, it is difficult to separate out the effects of prenatal drug exposure from social variables that often accompany it. Cognitive-behavioral theorists emphasize the role of parental modeling and reinforcement of antisocial traits in childhood. They also note that individuals with antisocial personality disorder tend to display impaired ability to connect actions with consequences. Psychodynamic theorists link antisocial tendencies with experiences of chaotic and abusive early experiences, and eventual identification with the aggressor as a defense mechanism.
  - o Borderline personality disorder involves unstable relationships over time, poor self-image, and impulsivity. Individuals with this diagnosis are often considered particularly difficult to treat because of their tendency to engage in self-destructive behavior. One of the central characteristics of the disorder is an intense fear of being abandoned. Research consistently demonstrates that many individuals with borderline personality disorder experienced physical or sexual abuse as children. Theories explaining this disorder focus on splitting (psychodynamic), and dichotomous thinking (cognitive), which leads to extreme interpretations of events.

A promising new treatment for individuals with borderline personality disorder is DBT, dialectical behavioral therapy.

o   Histrionic personality disorder is diagnosed when an individual is interpersonally superficial, overly dramatic, and attention seeking. Psychodynamic theorists view the emotional insecurity of these individuals as a product of disturbed early relation-ships, while cognitive-behavioral theorists suggest that they fear they cannot care for themselves and engage in such dramatic behaviors in order to influence others to provide the care and attention they need.

o   Individuals who are diagnosed with narcissistic personality disorder demonstrate grandiosity, crave admiration from others, and generally have little empathy for others. Psychodynamic therapists assert that a deep internal feeling of inadequacy leads to this disorder. Cognitive-behavioral focus on distorted, extreme self-evaluation, both positive and negative.

- **Cluster C**, consists of the anxious or fearful personality disorders. These are the avoidant, dependent, and obsessive-compulsive personality disorders.

  o   Avoidant personality disorder is diagnosed when an individual experiences extreme shyness or social inhibition and feelings of inadequacy. Individuals with this disorder generally would like to connect with others but they are overly concerned about being rejected and typically avoid any interactions where they *might* be criticized or rejected. Psychodynamic theorists posit that these individuals likely experienced heightened shame and anxiety in childhood, and suggest they learned to withdraw from others or to escape into fantasy. Cognitive-behavioral therapists work to help these individuals notice positive feedback instead of focusing only on the expected, negative feedback, and to develop a greater tolerance for difficult emotions.

  o   Dependent personality disorder consists of submissive, emotionally dependent behavior and the wish or expectation that others will make all decisions and take responsibility for the individual. Similar to other personality disorders, theorists place substantial emphasis on childhood experiences of individuals who develop this disorder. Cognitive-behavioral therapists suggest that parents likely reinforced early "needy" behavior leading to current behavior patterns, whereas psychodynamic theorists focus on problematic parent-child relationships. Biological theorists have noted the association between this disorder and "slow to warm up" temperament.

  o   Obsessive-compulsive personality disorder is diagnosed when an individual is preoccupied with perfectionism, order, and control. Psychodynamic theorists emphasize the role of defense mechanisms such as reaction formation, undoing, and isolation of affect in their explanation of this disorder. Cognitive-behavioral theorists note these individuals tendency to overfocus on details and thus miss the "big picture."

- Treatment outcomes for individuals with personality disorders have not generally been very successful but single-design studies and controlled outcome studies have indicated positive results for the treatment of some of personality disorders.

Classification in demographic context
- Personality disorders are not diagnosed until after the age of 18.
- A controversy in the diagnosis of some personality disorders has centered on a potential gender bias. Clinicians appear more likely to diagnose women who personality disorders seem typically feminine (e.g., borderline, histrionic, and dependent) and to diagnosis men with personality disorders that seem more typically masculine (e.g., paranoid, antisocial, narcissistic, etc.)
- Although most of the personality disorders occur at similar rates across different classes, antisocial and perhaps borderline personality disorders appear to be diagnosed at higher rates among individuals in lower socioeconomic group.

Cultural and historical relativism *in defining and classifying personality disorders*
- The historical relativism of personality disorders diagnoses becomes clear when one reviews the substantial changes in norms for social behavior over time. Cultural ***context*** is also very important; different cultures hold different standards for what is considered to be normal and abnormal interpersonal behavior.

*The **advantages and limitations** of the DSM-IV TR personality disorder diagnoses*
- Personality disorders have demonstrated relatively weak validity and reliability and thus it is important to consider the advantages and disadvantages of assigning these diagnoses. Some theorists have argued that a dimensional rather than a categorical diagnostic system would improve the accuracy of personality disorder diagnoses.

Key Terms

- Personality traits p. 351
- Ego-dystonic p. 352
- Ego-syntonic p. 352
- Personality disorders p. 352
- Personality p. 352
- Paranoid personality disorder p. 353
- Schemas p. 356
- Projection p. 357
- Schizoid personality disorder p. 358
- Temperament p. 359
- Withdrawal p. 359
- Intellectualization p. 359
- Schizotypal personality disorder p. 360
- Psychotic p. 360
- Ideas of reference p. 361
- Magical thinking p. 361
- Antisocial personality disorder p. 362
- Identification with the aggressor p. 365
- Borderline personality disorder p. 365
- Splitting p. 367
- Histrionic personality disorder p. 369
- Repression p. 370

Concept Questions

- What is a personality trait? How do we assess whether a trait is maladaptive?
- How do people with schizotypal personality disorder differ from individuals diagnosed with schizophrenia?
- What explanations do psychodynamic therapists offer for the development of paranoid personality disorder?
- Why is therapeutic alliance often difficult to establish with individuals with personality disorders?
- What is the possible role of temperament in the development of schizoid or schizotypal personality disorders? What perspective suggests that temperament is critical to the development of these disorders?
- What is intellectualization?
- What is the difference between schizoid and schizotypal personality disorders?
- What is magical thinking?
- What is the typical focus of cognitive behavioral interventions with individuals with schizotypal personality disorder?
- What are the primary characteristics of individuals with antisocial personality disorder?
- What is the evidence for a biological explanation of antisocial disorder?
- What factors do cognitive-behavioral theorists focus on when explaining antisocial tendencies?
- What is identification with the aggressor?
- Why are close relationships important to individuals with borderline personality disorder? What happens when they perceive a potential threat to the relationship?
- What are some explanations for "acting out" behavior observed in individuals with borderline personality disorder?

- What is splitting?
- What is DBT?
- How would you describe an individual with histrionic personality disorder? How would a cognitive-behavioral therapist generally work with such an individual?
- What is devaluation? Why might someone rely on this defense mechanism?
- How are people with narcissistic personality disorder similar to individuals with antisocial tendencies? How are they different?
- How do various theorists explain the development of dependent personality disorder?
- Why do psychodynamic therapists pay particular attention to transference when working with individuals with dependent personality disorder?
- What is reaction formation? How do individuals with obsessive-compulsive personality disorder employ this defense mechanism?
- How are uncontrolled studies different from single-case studies?
- What is the relevance of age to the diagnosis of a personality disorder?
- Why has there been some suggestion of a gender bias in the diagnosis of personality disorders?
- What are the differences between a dimensional and a categorical diagnostic system?

Multiple-Choice Questions

1. Larry's cognitive-behavioral therapist is concerned about his new client's tendency to think others are out to get him. Larry has been coming to therapy for about a month and it is apparent that he thinks his colleagues at work are trying to undermine him. He also thinks his landlady is spying on him. Which personality disorder diagnosis is Larry most likely to receive?
   A. paranoid
   B. schizoid
   C. schizotypal
   D. narcissistic
   Ans. A

2. Which of the following strategies is Larry's therapist most likely to employ?
   A. thoroughly explore Larry's childhood to learn if he had repeated experiences of humiliation and ridicule that led him to suspect the intentions of others
   B. directly challenge Larry's faulty beliefs about his colleagues' and landlady's behavior
   C. help Larry to evaluate the actual threat and likelihood of harm from his colleagues and landlady so that he can reduce some of his suspicions and then evaluate his assumptions about others
   D. identify the ways in which Larry has been reinforced for being suspicious of others and extinguish those responses using contingency therapy
   Ans. C

3. Some theorists have suggested that schizotypal personality disorder is similar to _____ in terms of the expression of odd beliefs and behaviors, but that it is a much less severe disorder, specifically because individuals with schizotypal personality disorder generally have a greater awareness of reality.
   A. schizoid personality disorder
   B. schizophrenia
   C. paranoid personality disorder
   D. avoidant personality disorder
   Ans. B

4. According to your textbook, cognitive-behavioral therapists have argued that antisocial personality disorder is linked to
   A. violence on television
   B. faulty beliefs that others are out to get you, so you better not let them get too close
   C. parental modeling of negative behaviors and reinforcement for antisocial traits
   D. a clear, manipulative ability to connect actions with consequences
   Ans. C

5. Cody is in a group that focuses on mindfulness, teaching new behaviors for managing crises, challenging misinterpretations of others' intentions, and increasing control over emotions. She is most likely in a group based on _____.
   A. dialectical behavioral therapy
   B. cognitive-behavioral therapy
   C. contingency therapy
   D. interpersonal therapy
   Ans. A

6. Ted is in therapy because he is having difficulty getting along with his wife. They are fighting about how he treats their children and whether he is "too picky." He has always been very tidy, but since they had children, he has been demanding that everything be put back in its proper place and he can't seem to understand why his 2 and 4-year old children do not follow his directions and maintain the house the way he wishes. He thinks they may be trying to provoke him because when he gets upset, his wife lets them have their way. Ted most likely would meet the criteria for
   A. narcissistic personality disorder
   B. obsessive-compulsive personality disorder
   C. dependent personality disorder
   D. paranoid personality disorder
   Ans. B

7. In general, there are no class differences in the rate of diagnosis of the personality disorders, except for _____.
   A. narcissistic personality disorder
   B. paranoid personality disorder
   C. schizotypal personality disorder
   D. antisocial personality disorder
   Ans. D

Short-Answer Essay Questions

1. How do we distinguish between a normal personality trait and a personality disorder? When do personality traits lead to a diagnosis of a personality disorder?

2. How do cognitive-behavioral therapists explain the development of a personality disorder? What interventions might a cognitive-behavioral therapist use with an individual who has paranoid personality disorder or with an individual with obsessive-compulsive personality disorder?

3. Describe the Cluster A personality disorders and discuss the central features of each. How do we distinguish among them?

4. How does the psychodynamic concept of identification with the aggressor explain antisocial behavior?

5. Molly is 38 years of age and has self referred for therapy after the breakup of her most recent engagement. Over the past six years, Molly has been engaged three times and each time, has experienced a breakup within weeks of the wedding date. She is well dressed in a coordinated miniskirt outfit, tall boots, and matching accessories. She is an attractive, engaging woman. She describes her heartbreak over the recent breakup and seems very distraught but also displays anger at her fiancé's betrayal of her. She explains she is seeking help because she always falls for "bad guys." Molly indicates that she has "gal pals" whom she shops with and meets for coffee but feels like she cannot confide in any of them when she is upset or needs support. That is part of why it seems so important to find "Mr. Right" instead of these "Mr. Wrongs." Molly also describes a history of varied career interests. She appears to have been successful in several different jobs for a time and then to have had "trouble" with her bosses. Currently, she is unemployed. Molly also describes periods in the past where she has been very depressed and has wanted to die, usually just after a breakup. When asked why she has wanted to die, Molly describes feeling alone and empty and sometimes being uncertain about whether she is "real." What diagnosis would you give Molly and why? Are there any additional diagnoses you would consider pending additional information? Discuss your reasoning.

6. According to theorists from the biological perspective, how is temperament involved in the development of some personality disorders?

7. Describe the criteria for schizoid and avoidant personality disorder. How do these disorders differ?

8. Do you think there is a gender bias in the diagnosis of personality disorders? Could we remove or work to eliminate criteria that we consider specifically masculine or feminine from the descriptions of personality disorders and still have viable criteria sets?

9. Compare and contrast cognitive-behavioral and psychodynamic explanations of borderline personality disorder.

10. What are the advantages and limitations of the current diagnoses for personality disorders?

Chapter 12
Psychosis and Schizophrenia

Learning Objectives

Defining psychosis and schizophrenia
- One defining feature of schizophrenia is the experience of psychosis, a substantial impairment in orientation to reality. Although psychosis can occur with other disorders, it is most frequently associated with schizophrenia.
- Delusions and hallucinations are the most common forms of psychosis. Delusions are false, distorted beliefs that are often bizarre in content, such as the belief that one is an alien savior of the world.
- Hallucinations are sensory experiences that feel real but are not related to actual stimuli in the environment. Individuals with schizophrenia typically report auditory hallucinations such as hearing voices calling to them or giving them instructions.
- Schizophrenia is a complex disorder that experts are still attempting to understand and explain.

Classifying psychosis and schizophrenia
- Schizophrenia consists of severe cognitive and behavioral symptoms which last more than six months and cause significant impairment. Symptoms are grouped as either positive (excesses) or negative (deficits).
- Some examples of positive symptoms include delusions, hallucinations, disorganized speech, and erratic behavior.
- Some examples of negative symptoms include flat affect, lack of motivation, and poverty of speech.
- Five subtypes of schizophrenia are included in the *DSM-IV-TR*.
  - Paranoid schizophrenia involves prominent delusions (especially delusions of persecution).
  - Disorganized schizophrenia is the subtype that involves confused speech, chaotic behavior, and/or disorganized thinking.
  - Catatonic schizophrenia is diagnosed when the predominant feature of the psychosis is psychomotoric—extremely slowed down movement, agitated movement, or lack of responsiveness to the environment.
  - Undifferentiated schizophrenia is the term used when an individual shows symptoms of more than one subtype or does not clearly fit one subtype of schizophrenia.
  - An individual who is no longer actively psychotic, but shows remaining signs of schizophrenia (such as negative symptoms) is diagnosed with residual schizophrenia.
- Individuals with schizophrenic-like symptoms that do not meet the full criteria for schizophrenia may have one of the disorders on the "schizophrenia spectrum."
  - Schizophreniform disorder is diagnosed when symptoms of schizophrenia appear for at least one month but have not been present for more than six months.
  - Brief psychotic disorder is diagnosed when psychotic symptoms have been present for less than a month.

- o Delusional disorder is a diagnosis which conveys that the individual has delusions or distorted beliefs (although not bizarre in content) but does not show the other symptoms of schizophrenia.
- o Shared delusional disorder is applied when two individuals in a close relationship share the same delusion(s).
- o Schizoaffective disorder describes individuals with symptoms of schizophrenia who also meet criteria for a mood disorder such as major depression.

Classification in demographic context
- The prevalence rate of schizophrenia is about 1% worldwide, but there are some differences in the rate of diagnosis in different demographic groups. In particular, individuals from lower economic groups who live in urban environments are at greater risk for schizophrenia.
- Schizophrenia typically begins early in adulthood, although it can begin in childhood or later in life.

Explaining and treating schizophrenia
- Schizophrenia generally involves three phases: prodromal (developing), active (psychotic), and residual (not psychotic but still having symptoms).
- The most common course for schizophrenia is one of chronic symptoms and a decline in functioning over time.
- Women tend to have a later onset, better pre-morbid functioning, fewer negative symptoms, and better prognosis than men.
- Evidence regarding brain functioning, structural abnormalities in the brain, and neuro-physiological abnormalities suggest a biological basis for schizophrenia.
- For many years, schizophrenia researchers focused on the role of dopamine and its association with positive symptoms in schizophrenia. However, the dopamine hypothesis no longer appears sufficient, and most scientists agree that there appear to be several neuro-transmitter and structural abnormalities in schizophrenic individuals.
- There is substantial evidence that individuals can have a genetic predisposition to schizophrenia. The biological environment appears to be influential as well, given research linking viruses, toxins, drug use, and prenatal injuries to the occurrence of schizophrenia.
- The introduction of antipsychotic medications in the 1950s helped manage the positive symptoms of individuals with schizophrenia and resulted in the release of many formerly hospitalized patients into the community (deinstitutionalization).
- However, the phenothiazines had many serious side effects and, in addition, communities were ill-prepared to care for the individuals released from the hospitals.
- Newer, "atypical" antipsychotic drugs are showing promise in their ability to help with both positive and negative symptoms of schizophrenia with fewer side effects, but relatively little is known about the long-term effects of these drugs.
- Some efforts are under way to prevent the onset of schizophrenia by treating individuals at high risk of developing the disorder *before* they show signs of impairment or psychosis.
- In general, psychodynamic theorists seem to believe that biological and psychological factors are influential in the development of schizophrenia and agree that psychotherapy is a useful additional component to medication.
- Fromm-Riechman, a psychodynamic theorist, theorized that a cold, overprotective, and demanding mother could cause schizophrenia. Although this theory is no longer accepted,

family theorists have noted some pathological patterns of relating in families of schizophrenic individuals.

- Cognitive theorists have noted that overattention (difficulty screening out irrelevant stimuli) and underattention (inability to attend to important stimuli) seem associated with positive and negative symptoms of schizophrenia. Some healthy relatives of schizophrenic individuals seem to have similar attentional problems.
- Behavioral interventions with schizophrenic individuals are based on the principles of operant conditioning and include token economies and social skills training.
- Sociocultural theories suggest that schizophrenia is influenced by institutional and social forces such as poverty. Milieu therapy and integrated community therapy were developed to provide social and community support in the treatment of schizophrenic individuals.
- Schizophrenia is best explained by a combination of theories and thus clearly illustrates the *principle of multiple causality*.

Key Terms

- Psychosis p. 393
- Hallucinations p. 393
- Delusions p. 393
- Dementia praecox p. 395
- Schizophrenia p. 397
- Disorganized speech p. 398
- Grossly disorganized behavior p. 398
- Positive symptoms (Type I) p. 398
- Negative symptoms (Type II) p. 399
- Loose associations p. 402
- Neologisms p. 402
- Clang associations p. 402
- Echolalia p. 402
- Echopraxia p. 402
- Word salad p. 402
- Catatonic p. 404
- Waxy flexibility p. 404
- Affective flattening p. 405
- Alogia /poverty of speech p. 405
- Thought blocking p. 405
- Avolition p. 405
- Anhedonia p. 405
- Downward drift p. 405
- Paranoid schizophrenia p. 406
- Disorganized schizophrenia p. 406
- Catatonic schizophrenia p. 406
- Undifferentiated schizophrenia p. 406
- Residual schizophrenia p. 406
- Schizophrenia spectrum p. 407
- Schizoaffective disorder p. 407

Concept Questions

- What are the differences between hallucinations and delusions? Give an example of each.
- Why is it important to take *context* into account when determining if a belief is a delusion?
- Historically, how did experts learn to distinguish schizophrenia from other disorders with psychosis? For example, what are the typical characteristics of schizophrenia in comparison to bipolar disorder?
- How do positive symptoms differ from negative symptoms?
- Give some examples of different types of delusions. Which are most common?
- What symptoms illustrate disturbed thinking or speech processes in schizophrenia?
- What is "word salad"? Does this form of communication have any meaning?

- What are typical negative symptoms of schizophrenia?
- Which symptoms—positive or negative—do you think most influence an individual's functioning? If you put yourself in the position of someone with schizophrenia, which of these symptoms do you think would be most debilitating?
- What is the long-term prognosis for most individuals with schizophrenia? What is the likelihood of recovery?
- What is the primary distinction between schizophreniform disorder and schizophrenia?
- Who is most at risk of schizophrenia and why?
- What is the most common course for an individual with schizophrenia?
- What is the dopamine hypothesis? How do the side effects of dopamine treatments for individuals with Parkinson's disease support this hypothesis?
- What are possible reasons for the higher rate of schizophrenia in individuals born in the winter?
- How do concordance rates help us to understand the influence of genes versus the environment in schizophrenia?
- What was "deinstitutionalization"? What have the long-term consequences been of this policy?
- How do the new, atypical antipsychotic drugs differ from the phenothiazines?
- Do you favor the idea of treating individuals at high risk of developing schizophrenia before they show any signs of impairment or psychosis? What are the potential benefits of such an approach? Disadvantages?
- Describe the cognitive concepts of overattention and underattention.
- What does research suggest about patterns of communication in families of schizophrenic individuals?

Multiple-Choice Questions

1. Which of the following is a delusion?
   A. Alfred thinks of his sister telling him what to do to guide him through his day.
   B. John worries that he has a tumor even though his doctor says he probably does not.
   C. Susan notices when people wear blue accessories and believes that these articles of clothing are signs that these individuals mean her harm.
   D. Tyler hears voices telling him to run away when he watches ESPN highlights.
   Ans. C

2. David believes that the patterns formed by smoke from factories are symbols of the state of the world. If the smoke curls in, toward itself, he believes this is a special sign of impending doom. David is demonstrating which of the following?
   A. hallucination
   B. delusion of grandeur
   C. hypochondrial illusions
   D. delusion of reference
   Ans. D

3. Individuals with disorganized schizophrenia
   A. are most likely to recover
   B. have predominant delusions of grandeur
   C. tend to have a poor prognosis
   D. tend to be immobile and unresponsive to the environment
   Ans. C

4. Which of the following individuals is least likely to recover fully from his or her disorder?
   A. an individual with disorganized schizophrenia in Pakistan
   B. an individual with disorganized schizophrenia in the United States
   C. an individual with paranoid schizophrenia in England
   D. an individual with brief psychotic disorder in Canada
   Ans. B

5. Which of the following offers support for the dopamine hypothesis?
   A. the association between psychosis and a lack of dopamine at D2 receptor sites
   B. the association between negative symptoms and excess dopamine at D2 receptor sites
   C. the association between positive symptoms and a lack of dopamine at D2 receptor sites
   D. the association between positive symptoms and an excess of dopamine at D2 receptor sites
   Ans. D

6. Which of the following individuals has the greatest likelihood of developing schizophrenia?
   A. someone born in the winter
   B. someone who lives in poverty
   C. someone who is the monozygotic twin of an individual with schizophrenia
   D. someone who is the first-degree relative of an individual with schizophrenia
   Ans. C

7. Tardive dyskenesia is
   A. an irreversible condition consisting of involuntary movements
   B. a theory that examines behaviors which resemble symptoms of schizophrenia
   C. extreme muscle rigidity and elevated temperature
   D. a form of biological treatment for schizophrenia
   Ans. A

8. When his mother came to visit, Sam greeted her with a handshake. She asked, "What's the matter, don't you love your mother?" When Sam moved to give her a hug instead, his mother became rigid and pushed him away. Mrs. Jones' behavior is an example of
   A. schizophreniform disorder
   B. double-bind communication
   C. expressed emotion
   D. catatonic behavior
   Ans. B

Short-Answer Essay Questions

1. What are some of the myths about schizophrenia?

2. Why is it important to develop uniform or standardized criteria for a disorder? Discuss the evolution of the diagnosis of schizophrenia and, in particular, note problems with the lack of clarity in the meaning of the term schizophrenia.

3. Identify and describe three different types of delusions.

4. Compare and contrast paranoid schizophrenia, delusional disorder, and paranoid personality disorder (Chapter 11). What key features help to distinguish among these three diagnoses?

5. Alex has been acting strangely. For the past three months, his behavior has been getting progressively more bizarre. At first, he just seemed more withdrawn and uncomfortable around others. Now, he is convinced that his neighbors are listening to him when he talks on the phone and that they are monitoring his dreams. He generally refuses to speak, and when he does he seems to have a limited vocabulary. He has also stopped taking care of himself; he is dirty and not eating well. When he does interact with others, he swings his arms back and forth rapidly, as if to make certain others do not get too close. Finally, he seems convinced that the earth is imploding on itself and is preparing for the temperature to rise until the planet burns up from the inside out. What diagnosis would you give Alex? Why is the length of time he has had his symptoms an important consideration for your diagnosis? Identify at least two positive symptoms and two negative symptoms in your discussion.

6. What is "downward drift?" How is this concept relevant to the prognosis of individuals with schizophrenia?

7. Discuss findings of structural abnormalities in the brains of schizophrenic individuals. How does this evidence provide support for a biological perspective on schizophrenia? What are some problems with this evidence?

8. What are some of the advantages of biological interventions for schizophrenia? What are possible disadvantages?

9. What is "personal therapy?" What is the primary focus of this intervention for schizophrenia?

10. What is "expressed emotion?" Why would a family therapist work to decrease high levels of expressed emotion in the family of an individual with schizophrenia?

Chapter 13

Lifespan Development: Disorders of Childhood and Old Age

Learning Objectives

Defining disorders of childhood
- Abnormal behavior in children has received less attention than abnormal behavior in adults. This is due in part to our difficulty defining abnormal behavior at different ages; behavior that is normal at age 2 clearly differs dramatically from normal behavior at age 6 or 11.
- Anna Freud, and subsequently many others, define child psychopathology as an interference with normal, progressive development. This means **context** is very important; we must consider what developmentally appropriate behavior is for a given child within the **context** of his/her age. In addition, we must be aware of the **continuum between abnormal and normal behavior**; most children display some disruptive behavior at times. Only behaviors that interfere with progressive development are considered abnormal. Developmental psychopathology is a subfield of psychology that considers childhood behavior within its developmental **context**.

Classifying, explaining, and treating disorders of childhood
- Mental retardation is diagnosed when an individual shows significantly impaired intellectual functioning as evidenced by an IQ below 70, and substantial deficits in two or more basic skills such as self-care, communication/social skills, work, health, or safety. This disorder is noted on Axis II because it lasts throughout an individual's life. Mental retardation is categorized as mild, moderate, severe, or profound.
  - Mental retardation is usually caused by genetic abnormalities. Down syndrome or trisomy 21 is the most common genetic cause of mental retardation followed by Fragile X syndrome. Mental retardation can also be caused by metabolic deficiencies, such as PKU, and prenatal and postnatal complications. Fetal alcohol syndrome is caused by consumption of alcohol during pregnancy. Shaking an infant such that there is severe bruising of the brain and heavy bleeding in the skull causes shaken baby syndrome. This syndrome, usually caused by a frustrated and over-whelmed caregiver, is the most common childhood event (post-birth) associated with mental retardation. Family or sociocultural factors such as extreme deprivation of stimulation and/or experiences associated with poverty, including malnutrition, substandard education, and low parental involvement can also cause mental retardation.
  - Interventions for mentally retarded children focus on normalization the effort to promote the most normal functioning possible. These children usually receive special education or are placed in inclusive classrooms.
- Children with learning disorders have normal overall intelligence but are deficient in a specific skill such as reading, math, or writing. The biological perspective identifies genetic influences and brain abnormalities as the two primary causes of learning disorders. Many children diagnosed with learning disorders also meet criteria for attention deficit hyperactivity disorder (ADHD). Family systems theorists note that families and schools can

have negative interaction with one another, leading to learning deficits in children. For example, this occurs when families do not engage in early learning activities (such as reading to their children) and schools consequently assume that children from these families are less intelligent rather than simply under prepared for school. Although many causes of learning disorders are assumed to be biological, interventions are typically behavioral and cognitive.

- The category of pervasive developmental disorders consists of conditions defined by severe, chronic impairment in many areas of functioning.
    - o Autism is the most common of these disorders and is broadly characterized by delayed or absent language, impaired social skills, a lack of interest in social relationships, and repetitive behavior. Other disorders in this category include Asperger's disorder, Rett's disorder (girls only), and childhood disintegrative disorder.
    - o Although we do not know the exact cause of autism, the biological perspective is central to our understanding of this disorder. The evidence for a genetic cause of autism is extremely strong; concordance rates for identical twins are above 90%. Research has found some differences between autistic and nonautistic individuals regarding specific prenatal and birth factors, such as prematurity, neuroanatomical anomalies, and levels of serotonin, but none of this research is definitive. Biological interventions, specifically different medications to assist with agitated behavior or emotional reactivity, have been helpful, but no single medication works for all autistic individuals. Behavioral interventions have been very effective and are widely used with autistic individuals. Shaping techniques have been used to teach desired behaviors, and existing early intervention programs include the Lovaas and TEACCH programs.
- One of the most commonly diagnosed disorders in children is attention deficit/hyperactivity disorder (ADHD). To be diagnosed with this disorder, a child must demonstrate symptoms of inattention (not listening, not following instructions), hyperactivity (excessive motor activity, fidgeting, excessive talking), and impulsivity (interrupts or blurts out) before age 7. Roughly 30% of children diagnosed with this disorder no longer have the symptoms by adulthood, whereas the 70% continue to experience ADHD and are more likely to have interpersonal problems, to engage in antisocial behavior, and to abuse substances.
    - o ADHD may be related to biological factors. Some children with ADHD appear to have congenital abnormalities in the frontal and striatal regions of the brain; 57% of children born to adults with ADHD also meet criteria for the disorder. Biological interventions with ADHD are very common. Stimulants such as Ritalin appear to help children to focus their attention, although typical side effects include insomnia and appetite suppression.
    - o Psychodynamic theorists have noted that children can display ADHD-like symptoms when they are experiencing emotional distress. Thus, they advocate assessing whether the symptoms occur across different situations and attending to the *context* in which symptoms emerged.
    - o Behavioral and cognitive techniques have been combined to help target and reinforce particular behaviors and to help correct faulty assumptions of parents and children about the meaning of various symptoms. In general, behavioral interventions appear effective while they are being applied but do not seem to last beyond the length of

the intervention. Research studies suggest that treatments combining medication and behavioral techniques are most effective and well received by families and teachers.

- Oppositional defiant disorder (ODD) involves behaviors such as losing one's temper, defying rules, arguing with adults, blaming others, and being resentful of others for at least four months. These behaviors occur at the extreme end of the ***continuum between normal and abnormal behavior***. It is very important to take into account whether these behaviors are developmentally appropriate (e.g., the terrible twos) or if they are interfering with development.
    - o There is high comorbidty between ODD and ADHD. A quarter of the children diagnosed with ODD eventually develop conduct disorder (CD), which consists of the violation of others' rights, including aggression toward others. Many individuals who receive this diagnosis engage in antisocial behavior as adults.
    - o Sociocultural theorists have noted that children living in poor, high-crime neighborhoods are at heightened risk for developing ODD or CD. Research on family variables has found associations between ODD and CD and harsh, inconsistent parental discipline, low parental warmth and acceptance, and parental rewards for disruptive behavior. Sociocultural interventions include teaching skills such as positive resolution of conflicts and other prosocial behaviors.
    - o Cognitive theorists have noted that children with ODD and CD tend to assume others' intentions are hostile and to develop aggressive resolutions to problems. Cognitive therapists work to help children make more realistic attributions about others' intentions and behaviors and to develop a broader array of problem-solving options (and consider the consequences of each option) before they act.
- Separation anxiety disorder is diagnosed when a child displays extreme anxiety when separated or anticipating separation from home or primary attachment figures. Some children develop these symptoms after a traumatic event. Psychodynamic theorists suggest that children can become clingy when struggling with their own rejecting or hostile impulses. Cognitive-behavioral interventions aim to help children manage their anxiety. Some genetic evidence suggests that SAD may have a biological component.
- It is important to consider the ***advantages and disadvantages of diagnoses*** of childhood disorders. Many of the diagnostic categories are relatively new and still lack good reliability and validity. Using additional resources such as behavioral checklists with multiple reporters or psychodynamic developmental profiles can provide important, supplemental information to *DSM* diagnoses.

Classification in demographic context
- o Many disorders of childhood are diagnosed only when children begin to attend school and can easily be compared with their peers.
- o The same psychological problem can be marked by different symptoms for children of different ages. For example, depression typically involves listlessness in infants, distractibility in young children, and irritability in teenagers.
- o Four out of five of the childhood disorders described in this chapter occur predominantly in boys, with SAD as the only exception.
- o Cultural-familial retardation results primarily from the effects of poverty on early childhood development.

Defining, classifying, explaining, and treating disorders of old age

- Delirium involves disturbances in attention with marked changes in cognitive abilities and a rapid onset of symptoms. Delirium is usually a temporary condition caused by a variety of medical conditions. Ten to 15% of adults are admitted to the hospital in a delirious state or develop delirium while hospitalized. Treatment consists of identifying and addressing the underlying cause of the delirium. Individuals with this disorder tend to do better when reassured by someone familiar and/or trusted. Symptoms, especially agitation, can increase later in the day—this is known as "sundowning"—and this effect can be addressed with light treatments.
- Dementia typically consists of a more gradual development of several cognitive difficulties including memory impairment as well as difficulty with language, recognition, or planning. Alzheimer's disease is the most common form of dementia. It is rare before age 50 but occurs in 20% of all people older than 85. Women are at greater risk for dementia, because they tend to live longer than men.
- Alzheimer's can only be conclusively diagnosed by autopsy, when there is evidence of neuretic plaques and neurofibrillary tangles. We do not yet know the exact cause of Alzheimer's disease. Studies of genetic contributions to this disease are complicated because the disease occurs late in life and currently is not detectable in living relatives. Additional causes of dementia include: cerebrovascular diseases, Huntington's disease, Parkinson's disease, and HIV disease.
- Treatment for dementia often includes placement in a residential center when intensive supervision is necessary, supportive services are often available for the caregivers of people suffering from dementia.

Key Terms

- Developmental psychopathology p. 438
- Maturationist p. 439
- Behaviorism p. 439
- Mental retardation p. 441
- Down syndrome p. 442
- Trisomy 21 p. 442
- Fragile X syndrome p. 443
- Phenylketonuria (PKU) p. 443
- Tay-Sachs disease p. 443
- Fetal alcohol syndrome p. 443
- Shaken baby syndrome p. 443
- Normalization p. 444
- Special education p. 444
- Inclusion classrooms p. 444
- Sheltered workshops p. 444
- Learning disorders p. 445
- Dyslexia p. 446
- Dysgraphia p. 446
- Dyscalculia p. 446

Concept Questions

- Why is *context* so important in defining abnormal behavior in childhood?
- What criteria seem most useful in determining when behavior is abnormal during childhood?
- How do the maturationist and behaviorist explanations of child development differ?
- What are the different levels of mental retardation? Which level of functioning is most common?
- What is the controversy surrounding the use of special education versus inclusive classrooms?
- What are some different types of learning disorders? How do we design interventions for learning disorders?
- What are the *advantages and disadvantages* of our current diagnostic system when assessing learning disorders?
- What is the difference between autism and Asperger's syndrome?
- What does savant mean? How common are savant skills?
- Describe childhood disintegrative disorder. When do caregivers typically begin to see signs of this disorder?
- Who is Temple Grandin? Why is she unusual?
- What is the evidence for a biological explanation of autism? Do we know what causes autism?

- What types of interventions are most commonly used with autistic individuals?
- What are the criticisms of the early intervention program by Lovaas? Do you agree or disagree with these critiques?
- What explanation for autism did psychodynamic theorists offer in the 1960s? How do you think this theory affected families of autistic individuals?
- What types of symptoms must a child display to be diagnosed with ADHD?
- According to research studies, what are the long-term outcomes for children who do not "grow out" of a diagnosis of ADHD?
- Some individuals feel that if Ritalin helps a child, the child has ADHD. Is this a helpful approach to diagnosis? Why or why not?
- What is the difference between ODD and CD?
- Who is most at risk for developing ODD or CD?
- What types of cognitive distortions are common in children with disruptive behavior disorders?
- What is the reliability and validity of the childhood disorders?
- Who is most at risk of being diagnosed with a childhood disorder?
- What are common signs of delirium?
- What are the symptoms of dementia?
- Which type of dementia is most common?
- What is the genetic evidence for Alzheimer's disease? What are the problems associated with studying the genetic heritability of this disease?
- What diseases or conditions other than Alzheimer's cause dementia?
- Who is in the "sandwich generation" and why are we concerned about the stresses placed on them?

Multiple-Choice Questions

1. Which of the following methods is the most useful in determining when behavior is abnormal in children?
   A. when they engage in help seeking
   B. when behavior is deviant
   C. when behavior interferes with normal development
   D. when behavior causes distress
   Ans. C

2. Tony is a friendly guy who sweeps the sidewalks in front of several stores each morning. He is very proud of his sweeping job. Tony lives in a supervised group home and attends a daily program where he receives substantial help managing his finances, and checks off goals related to self care and daily activities. Tony functions at about a second grade level. He most likely fits which of the following levels of mental retardation?
   A. mild
   B. moderate
   C. severe
   D. profound
   Ans. B

3. Children with reading disorders seem to rely on the _____ instead of the area usually used for reading, the posterior left hemisphere.
   A. frontal hemisphere
   B. occipital lobe
   C. parietal lobe
   D. Brock's area
   Ans. A

4. Charlie is three years old. He has excellent verbal skills, and likes to talk about dinosaurs (he can name all the dinosaurs and list their primary characteristics), but he seems very different from other children. He has never liked to be held or cuddled, although he does enjoy looking at books with his parents. He likes watching repetitive motions such as the automatic doors at stores. He does not like loud noises and cries if he is around a lot of activity such as if more than 2 or 3 other children are nearby. Based on this description, Charlie most likely fits which of the following diagnoses?
   A. Rett's disorder
   B. Asperger's disorder
   C. Autism
   D. childhood disintegrative disorder
   Ans. B

5. The clearest research evidence for the biological perspective regarding an explanation of autism is
   A. research identifying different levels of neurotransmitters in autistic and nonautistic children
   B. associations between various prenatal factors and autism
   C. associations between birth variables and autism
   D. research highlighting the very high concordance rate among identical twins
   Ans. D

6. Research thus far suggests that the most likely biological cause(s) of ADHD is/are
   A. brain damage
   B. high levels of dopamine
   C. congenital abnormalities in the frontal and striatal regions of the brain
   D. all of the above
   Ans. C

7. Children and adolescents who meet criteria for ODD and CD have shown which of the following general cognitive tendencies?
   A. believing others' intentions toward them are hostile
   B. generating predominantly aggressive resolutions to conflicts
   C. failure to consider the results of their behaviors
   D. all of the above
   Ans. D

8. Lately, Nancy has difficulty remembering things. Yesterday, when she went to the store, she could not focus on her errands and then had trouble figuring out how to get home. She finds she does much better in the morning, but in the past few days has been feeling irritable and disoriented in the afternoon. Nancy most likely is experiencing
   A. delirium
   B. Alzheimer's dementia
   C. vascular dementia
   D. Huntington's disease
   Ans. A

9. Alzheimer's disease is conclusively diagnosed
   A. on the basis of impaired cognitive functioning and memory loss
   B. when vascular dementia has been ruled out
   C. during autopsy, when there is evidence of neuretic plaques and neurofibrillary tangles
   D. when there is gradual degeneration of the caudate nucleus
   Ans. C

Short-Answer Essay Questions

1. What are the different causes of mental retardation? Which are preventable?

2. How does mental retardation differ from the pervasive developmental disorders? How is it similar?

3. Describe three pervasive childhood disorders and note the central features that allow us to distinguish among them.

4. What are the *advantages and limitations* of the ADHD diagnosis? Why is there a controversy about the increasing rates of diagnosis of this disorder?

5. Discuss the family systems and sociocultural perspectives on disruptive behavior disorders. What role do caregivers and communities play? What are possible points of intervention?

6. How would a cognitive therapist work with a child with ODD or CD? What would most likely be the main focus of the treatment?

7. What are some possible explanations for the fact that boys diagnosed with childhood disorders much more frequently than girls?

8. How do we differentiate between delirium and dementia? What are the primary interventions for each of these disorders?

Chapter 14
Psychological Stress and Physical Disorders

Learning Objectives

Psychophysiology: Defining psychological stress and categorizing stressors
- When we talk about stress, we are usually describing a negative reaction to an event or experience. However, stress is generally determined by the interaction between the person and his/her environment. In other words, an event that is very stressful to one person may not be stressful for another. Even the context of the event can influence whether it is stressful for the same person—you would probably be only mildly irritated with tripping or stumbling when you are out and about, but may feel very stressed about a similar misstep when crossing the stage during graduation.
- The degree of stress associated with an event is related to one's cognitive appraisal of the situation—specifically, whether the individual perceives the event to represent an immediate or distant threat and whether he/she has resources to cope with the event. In addition, events are generally more stressful if the individual perceives them to be: negative, uncontrollable, ambiguous, unpredictable, and/or requiring significant adaptation.
- Stressful events or stressors can be positive or negative life events that require significant change or just daily hassles. When an event requires greater adaptation or change, it is more likely to be stressful. However, even daily events such as traffic jams can contribute to emotional or physical symptoms related to stress.
- Ongoing chronic stress is related to difficult circumstances in everyday life such as coping with a long-term illness or lacking basic resources such as food or shelter.
- Stress also can be caused by extreme events such as catastrophes. The duration, proximity, and severity of an event as well as the psychological state of the individual prior to the event and the availability of social support after the event influence the degree to which the event is traumatic.

Explaining and treating psychophysiological disorders
- Physical disorders that are caused or worsened by stress are called psychophysiological illnesses. Three pathways describe how stress affects physical illnesses. First, stress can affect health-related behaviors, which can lead to illness. For example, many people change their eating, sleeping, and/or exercise habits when they are stressed. Next, stress can directly influence physiological reactions. Finally, personality traits may influence how one manages psychological stress and, subsequently, affect health-related behaviors and health outcomes.
- There are several theories about how the body responds to stress. These include flight-or-fight, general adaptation syndrome, and theories from the field of psychoneuroimmunology.
- Recent studies have demonstrated the relationship between stress and disease. For example, college students who reported higher levels of stress were more likely to get sick when exposed to viruses than their peers who reported lower levels of stress. Thus, stress combined with viral exposure (***principle of multiple causality***) contributes to illness.

- Cardiovascular reactivity is another example of how individuals vary in their response to stress. Volunteers who engage in stressful tasks such as the Stroop task or the cold pressor task experience different heart rates and blood pressure levels in the same situation. High reactors have a significant increase in heart rate and blood pressure, whereas low reactors do not. Studies such as these can help us to determine who is most at risk for heart attacks or other cardiovascular diseases.
- Smoking, obesity, lack of exercise, diabetes and a genetic predisposition to heart problems are all associated with coronary heart disease, as are some personality factors, especially hostility.
- Psychosocial stress also contributes to some illnesses such as asthma, cancer, and migraine headaches.
- Individuals who have a pessimistic cognitive explanatory style are more likely to become ill. This is probably because individuals with optimistic styles are more likely to engage in healthy activities because they believe that their actions will have a beneficial effect.
- Individuals who engage in repressive coping try to ignore or repress stress and appear content, but are making a great effort to keep their negative feelings under control.
- Several behavioral interventions are designed to help people cope with and manage stress. Relaxation training teaches people how to regulate their breathing and be more aware of sensations in their bodies. Yoga, with its focus on breathing and body awareness, appears to have beneficial effects on stress. Biofeedback teaches individuals how to control their autonomic physiological functions by providing feedback about involuntary functions such as heart rate or blood pressure. Biofeedback appears to be an effective aid in treating stress-related disorders such as asthma, migraine headaches, and insomnia.
- Cognitive-behavioral therapists work to help clients manage stress by engaging in cognitive retraining and working to change maladaptive explanatory styles.
- Social support can be instrumental (help with tasks), emotional (acceptance and listening), and informational. Social support appears to prevent illness and to improve outcome if a person does become ill.

Defining the somatoform disorders
- A somatoform disorder is diagnosed when an individual has physical symptoms in the absence of a medical disorder. In contrast, a factitious disorder is diagnosed when a person deliberately causes physical symptoms or even fakes them in order to convince others that he/she is sick.
- Conversion disorder, previously known as hysteria, consists of problems in motor or sensory functions that have no physiological cause. Often, individuals with this disorder appear strangely indifferent to their symptoms.
- Somatization disorder is diagnosed when an individual reports pains in multiple areas of his/her body, has experienced these pains for many years, and the pains are not the result of a medical condition or substance use.
- Pain disorder is diagnosed when there is physical pain or discomfort without a physiological cause.
- Hypochondriasis is extreme worry or fear that one has or will contract a serious disease.
- Like the other somatoform disorders, body dysmorphic disorder involves a focus on the body, but in this case the individual believes he/she has a physical defect and is preoccupied by this slight or imagined defect.

- Similar to other psychological disorders, the diagnosis of a somatoform disorder is made only if an individual appears to be in distress and/or is experiencing impaired functioning.

The advantages and disadvantages of somatoform diagnoses
- The somatoform disorders are grouped based on the shared characteristic of concern about the body; however, it is not clear that these disorders actually have similar psychological causes.

Classification in demographic context
- Although somatoform disorders are universal, the ways in which they are expressed vary across cultures and have changed over the course of history.
- Women are two to ten more times likely to be diagnosed with a conversion disorder than are men. However, rates of hypochondriasis and body dysmorphic disorder are similar in men and women.
- Diagnosis of somatoform disorders usually occurs in adolescence or adulthood. Somatization disorder and hypochondriasis occur more frequently in individuals who are uneducated and/or lacking in economic resources. Conversion disorder is also more common in less educated individuals, in rural populations, and among individuals with few economic resources.

Explaining and treating the somatoform disorders
- Psychodynamic theorists suggest that the physical symptoms or concerns experienced by individuals with somatoform disorders are indirect expressions of unconscious emotional distress. For example, these theorists suggest that conversion disorder occurs when individuals repress feelings that they cannot tolerate. Therapists from this perspective work to help clients recognize that they are using defense mechanisms such as repression or regression and to connect these mechanisms to their emotional distress.
- Behavioral theorists have proposed that modeling and reinforcement can lead to the development of somatoform disorders; however, only the influence of modeling has been strongly supported by empirical research.
- Cognitive theorists emphasize the role of cognitive distortions such as catastrophizing and amplification in the development of somatoform disorders. For example, they argue that individuals with hypochondriasis attend very closely to their bodies and perceive even minor sensations as intense (amplification) and then believe that these sensations signal serious problems (catastrophizing). Cognitive therapists use cognitive restructuring to change irrational and problematic beliefs as well as specific interventions such as exposure and response prevention.
- Many individuals who experience childhood sexual abuse or who are sexually assaulted as adults develop somatization disorder.
- People with somatoform disorders also often report anxiety and depression. Medications aimed at treating anxiety and mood symptoms can help alleviate somatic symptoms in some individuals.
- The relationship between hypnosis and the somatoform disorders illustrates the **connection between mind and body**. For example, some theorists suggest that individuals with conversion disorder have essentially hypnotized themselves into believing that they have lost specific physical functions.

Key Terms

- Psychophysiology p. 487
- Somatoform disorders p. 487
- Cognitive appraisal p. 488
- Stressors p. 489
- Life events p. 489
- Social Readjustment Rating Scale p. 489
- Chronic stress p. 491
- Daily hassles p. 492
- Prospective study p. 492
- Catastrophes p. 492
- Trauma p. 492
- Posttraumatic stress disorder p. 493
- Psychophysiological disorders p. 494
- Flight-or-fight response p. 495
- General adaptation syndrome p. 495
- Psychoneuroimmunology p. 495
- Viral challenge studies p. 495
- Antigens p. 496
- Immunosuppression p. 496
- Hypertension p. 497
- Essential hypertension p.497
- Asthma p. 498
- Migraine headaches p. 498
- Cancer p. 498
- John Henryism p. 499
- Pessimism p. 500
- Optimism p. 500
- Repressive coping p. 501
- Relaxation training p. 502
- Biofeedback training p. 503
- Cognitive-behavioral stress management p. 504
- Somatoform disorders p. 506
- Factitious disorders p. 506
- Hysteria p. 506
- Conversion disorder p. 508
- Somatization disorder p. 509
- Pain disorder p. 511
- Hypochondriasis p. 512
- Body dysmorphic disorder p. 513
- Primary gain p. 518
- Secondary gain p. 518
- Repression p. 519
- Regression p. 519
- Modeling p. 519

- Reinforcement p. 519
- Amplification p. 519
- Exposure and response prevention p. 520
- Cognitive restructuring p. 521
- Comorbidity p. 522
- Autosuggestive disorder p.523

Concept Questions

- Define stress.
- Describe aspects or characteristics of an event that are linked with experiencing the event as stressful.
- What two factors tend to influence the extent to which events are appraised as stressful?
- What are the different types of events that can contribute to stress? Which do you think is more stressful—a significant life event or many everyday hassles? Why?
- Why are catastrophes almost always traumatic?
- What is the flight-or-fight response?
- What are viral challenge studies? What have these studies found? Based on these studies, what should *you* do to protect your health during inherently stressful times such as finals week?
- What is the Stroop task? How is it used in studies of stress?
- How does the ***principle of multiple causality*** apply to our understanding of the relationships among personality, stress, and health?
- What is a type A personality? What aspects of this personality place a person most at risk for developing a disease such as hypertension?
- What are some diseases that have been linked with psychosocial stress?
- What is a pessimistic explanatory style? How is explanatory style related to healthy and unhealthy behaviors?
- What are some behavioral techniques used to help individuals manage stress?
- How does cognitive retraining help to reduce stress?
- What are some of the ways social support appears to help individuals cope with stress?
- What is the difference between a somatoform disorder and a factitious disorder?
- What is Munchausen syndrome by proxy? Why might a caregiver engage in these behaviors?
- What is conversion disorder? When is someone most likely to develop conversion disorder?
- What is the difference between somatization disorder and pain disorder? What should a clinician do to assess whether the individual is presenting with psychological or medical problems?
- What is hypochondriasis? How might medical personnel address the concerns of individuals with hypochondriasis?
- What diagnostic criteria must be present to diagnose body dysmorphic disorder? If someone wants plastic surgery to change a part of his/her body, does this mean that person meets the criteria for body dysmorphic disorder?
- What are the ***advantages and limitations*** of the somatoform diagnoses?
- Based on demographic statistics, who is most likely to meet criteria for a conversion disorder?

- What is primary gain? How is it related to the development of a conversion disorder?
- What defense mechanisms do psychodynamic therapists believe to be involved in the development of somatoform disorders?
- According to behavioral theorists, what is the role of modeling and reinforcement in the development of somatoform disorders? Which of these concepts is best supported by research?
- Why would catastrophizing help maintain a disorder such as hypochondriasis?
- What is exposure and response prevention?
- What is the A-B-C-D-E format for a self-monitoring diary? What type of therapist would employ this technique?
- What is an autosuggestive disorder?

Multiple-Choice Questions

1. Which of the following events is most stressful according to the Social Readjustment Rating Scale?
   A. starting school
   B. fighting with your in-laws
   C. getting married
   D. trouble with the boss
   Ans. C

2. Which of the following characteristics of a catastrophe influence whether it is experienced as traumatic?
   A. duration
   B. severity
   C. proximity
   D. all of the above
   Ans. D

3. Jeff was in a car accident earlier today. Someone turning left hit him as he went through a green light. At first, he felt numb but then he jumped into action, called the police, his folks, and arranged for a tow truck. Jeff is currently in the _____ phase of the general adaptation syndrome.
   A. alarm
   B. resistance
   C. exhaustion
   D. depletion
   Ans. B

4. Noah always expects the worst. For example, he knows his grandfather and father died of heart attacks and he fully expects that he will as well.
   A. Noah is most likely to suffer from a stress related disease because he is pessimistic and thus is unlikely to engage in behaviors that may benefit his health.
   B. Noah appears to be engaging in repressive coping and thus is at greater risk of a heart attack himself.
   C. Noah is probably a "low reactor" and has nothing to worry about.
   D. Noah is probably hostile and it is his hostility that will lead to cardiovascular problems.
   Ans. A

5. Sarah is hooked up to a machine that indicates her current blood pressure as she describes a meeting she had with her boss last week. When the machine indicates her pressure is increasing, she stops talking and quietly focuses on calming herself down. This is an example of
   A. restructuring
   B. relaxation training
   C. meditation
   D. biofeedback
   Ans. D

6. Shelby sees the doctor at least once a month. He began having discomfort in his stomach several years ago and frequently feels sharp pains in his lower stomach that lead to nausea and vomiting. He often asks for pain medication to decrease his discomfort, because nothing else has seemed to help. The doctors cannot find any physical cause for his discomfort. Shelby most likely has
   A. conversion disorder
   B. somatization disorder
   C. pain disorder
   D. body dysmorphic disorder
   Ans. C

7. A preoccupation with fear of developing a serious disease or the belief that one has a life-threatening disease even when there is no medical evidence to support the belief is called
   A. conversion disorder
   B. hypochondriasis
   C. body dysphoria
   D. pain disorder
   Ans. B

8. Empirical research on behavioral theories of somatoform disorders suggests that
   _____ is strongly associated with the development of somatoform disorders.
   A. regression
   B. repression
   C. reinforcement
   D. modeling
   Ans. D

9. Jill's therapist has asked her to keep a daily journal and to note whenever she thinks about her nose. Specifically she is supposed to note what activated her concerns about her nose, what she thought, what feelings she experienced as a result of her beliefs, what alternative beliefs might be more accurate, and how she feels after considering the alternative explanations she has generated. Jill's therapist is mostly working from the _____ perspective and is using the _____ technique.
A. psychodynamic, uncovering
B. cognitive, exposure and response prevention
C. cognitive, A-B-C-D-E
D. behavioral, reinforcement
Ans. C

Short-Answer Essay Questions

1. Think about an event in your life that you considered moderately stressful. How would you describe the conditions of that event? Did you feel in control? Was the outcome predictable? Discuss specific conditions or characteristics of the event that you believe might have led you to perceive it as stressful.

2. Julie has been very upset. Last week, her best friend told her she is moving away. In response to this news, Julie has hardly eaten and has slept very poorly. Now, she does not feel well and is wondering if she caught the flu that has been going around. Discuss how the event, Julie's response, and her current illness might be explained by one or more of the pathways through which stress can contribute to physical illness.

3. What is cardiovascular reactivity? Discuss how studies of individuals' responses to the cold pressor task help us to understand development of diseases such as hypertension and coronary heart disease.

4. What is cognitive retraining? How does it work? What is the desired outcome?

5. Eliza went to her doctor because she cannot feel her left foot, starting right at the ankle, almost like she is wearing a "numbing, short sock." This numbness began shortly after she learned that her brother had been wounded while fighting as a reservist. He is coming home soon and Eliza is determined to be very brave and offer him her support. She does not appear overly concerned about her foot, but does not want anything to get in the way of taking care of her brother. What diagnosis would you consider for Eliza and why? What treatment or intervention would you use to help her with this problem?

6. What are some possible reasons for the rate of conversion disorders diagnosed in women versus men?

7. What are the cognitive processes of amplification and catastrophizing? How do these ways of thinking contribute to developing a somatoform disorder such as hypochondriasis?